Scriptures for the

*L*ent 2010
Celebrate the Risen Christ

Andy and Sally Langford

A Lenten Study Based on the Revised Common Lectionary

 **Abingdon Press**

A Lenten Study Based on the Revised Common Lectionary

CELEBRATE THE RISEN CHRIST
by Andy and Sally Langford

Copyright © 2009 by Abingdon Press

All readings taken from the Revised Common Lectionary © 1992 Consultation on Common Texts are used by permission.

ISBN-13: 978-0-687-65981-4

Manufactured in the United States of America

09 10 11 12 13 14 15 16 17 18—10 9 8 7 6 5 4 3 2 1

Contents

Introduction

"Come, let us walk in the light of the Lord!" (Isaiah 2:5)

Join us on a journey toward Jerusalem and new life. As you follow Jesus and his disciples to Jerusalem and the sites of Jesus' death and resurrection, you will journey out of your ordinary life into a wilderness spirituality and ultimately toward abundant and everlasting life. On this journey you will walk not only with Jesus and his followers but with other faithful travelers, too. You will read in Scripture how Abraham, Joshua, Moses, and the prophet Isaiah claimed the promises of God for themselves and future generations, including ours.

The apostle Paul and first-century Christians in many different congregations throughout the Roman Empire will also accompany you as you risk leaving safe, comfortable places to follow Jesus toward the kingdom of God. The whole of Scripture encourages you to engage in such a journey.

In his book *Alice in Wonderland*, Lewis Carroll wrote about Alice meeting the Cheshire Cat. Alice was at a crossroads and saw the Cheshire Cat in a tree. Alice asked the cat which road to take. The cat asked Alice where she was going. Alice replied that she was going in no direction in particular. The cat replied that in that case any road

would do. Unlike the Cheshire Cat, we believe that the roads we take matter. If you take the wrong road, you may find yourself in the dark woods and far from home. If you take the right path, however, you will discover Jesus Christ and those who followed him walking right beside you and pointing you toward a glorious home not built with human hands but eternal in the heavens.

Our journey is a Lenten journey. Lent began on Wednesday night, four days ago, on a day we call Ash Wednesday. Following grand and sometimes excessive parties (Mardi Gras, Shrove Tuesday, or Carnival), Christians around the world participated in a solemn ceremony. People knelt before the Creator of the universe and anointed one another with ashes, remembering that from dust we came and to dust we shall return. They committed themselves to spiritual disciplines to prepare for Easter.

For the next seven weeks, join us as we commit ourselves to a disciplined observance of the 40 days of Lent. As you move from winter into spring, from the ashes of repentance to the joy of resurrection, you will listen to the Word of God, reflect on your life, and discover God's call to you. In this season, you will witness how Jesus' ultimate sacrifice for you ended not in defeat but in victory over death.

Likewise, you will discover that your journey with Jesus to the cross will conclude not with death but with new life.

Our prayers are with you as you begin your Lenten journey. May this journey not only be a journey of your mind, in which you come to understand more fully these important biblical texts, but also a journey of your heart, in which you are brought into the very presence of the living Jesus Christ. When you arrive at the garden tomb on Easter, may you see and experience our Savior more fully than ever before.

Trust in God

Scriptures for Lent:
The First Sunday
Deuteronomy 26:1-11
Romans 10:8b-13
Luke 4:1-13

Lent has begun. The word *lent* comes from the Anglo-Saxon word for "spring," a season that features the shortening of nights and a lengthening of days. In our garden, we have planted beautiful wildflowers called Lenten roses. These hardy white flowers bloom early every spring as a hint of resurrection possibility amidst other still hibernating plants.

The forty days of Lent recall forty years of wandering in the wilderness in the story of Moses and the people of Israel; the forty days Elijah fasted in the wilderness; and, particularly, the forty days of Jesus' wilderness retreat, which followed his baptism by John. These forty days can also be a time of disciplined reflection, study, and preparation of our hearts and souls.

Do you remember the movie *Batman Begins*? Batman is the comic book hero who has no super powers but practices serious athletic discipline, dresses in black, drives a cool car, and works out of a cave under a mansion. In the movie, the young boy Bruce Wayne comes face to face with the terrors of the world. First, Wayne falls into a dark cave of bats. Then the boy witnesses the robbery and murder of his parents. Finally, Wayne watches as evil people wreak havoc on his beloved Gotham City.

Fear, anger, and despair threaten to destroy Bruce Wayne. He travels the world to escape the darkness, eventually being tempted to become violent and vengeful himself. Wayne chooses to use all of his strength, intellect, wealth, and a wide array of high-tech weapons to fight injustice. His turn-around began when his teacher passionately asked Wayne, "Are you ready to begin?" Wayne donned the black mask of Batman and took on the sinister forces that threaten good people.

"Are you ready to begin?" is God's ongoing question to us. In the midst of a dark season, when chaos seems to rule the world and sin remains pervasive, we are invited to travel from darkness to light. We may choose to conform to this world and its values or to heed God's call to be transformed.

We will recognize our inability to save ourselves and recognize our need for God. We may commit to keeping the Lenten disciplines, but almost all of us will fail. We suspect, as in years before, that Sally will not be able to withdraw from chocolate and that Andy will fail to keep up with his exercise program. The goal of Lent, however, is not to keep the disciplines perfectly but to put ourselves in the position to receive God's grace. Even when we are faithless, God remains faithful.

In our Scripture passage for today, we find Jesus in the wilderness, where he was tempted by the devil after forty days of prayer. Profound trust in God sustained Jesus during the days of prayer and at the time of temptation.

Trusting in God permeates all the Scripture passages for this week. Moses reminded the Israelites as they prepared to enter the Holy Land that they could trust God, the One who liberated them from slavery in Egypt. Paul wrote to the Roman Christians, who lived in the greatest and most corrupt city in the world, that everyone who calls on the name of the Lord will be saved.

May you hear this week that ours is a God who can be trusted to liberate us through the life, death, and resurrection of Jesus Christ.

WANDERING ARAMEANS
DEUTERONOMY 26:1-11

The Book of Deuteronomy records the witness of Moses as he led the people through the Sinai wilderness toward the Promised Land. Long associated with King Josiah's religious reforms in the seventh century before Christ, the whole book rehearses the history of God with the people of the covenant. This Scripture also challenges us to be faithful to God's covenant.

Picture the setting for Moses' challenge to the Israelites. The people of Israel had made one last stop after forty years of wandering in the wilderness. Following their exodus from Egypt and four decades of traveling through the desert, the people were ready to cross over the river Jordan into Canaan, the Promised Land. However, before the people traveled any further, Moses paused to give them final instructions: "After you have entered Canaan, and when you are settled and living off the land, do not forget that God has given you that land. Each year, as an act of remembrance, offer your first harvested fruits in thanksgiving to God. In the holy sanctuary, remember again the story of God's care."

Moses told the people to remember that just as God had been with them in the past, so too was God with them in the present and would be with them in the future.

In this desolate location, overlooking the Jericho oasis, Moses instructed the people as they saw in the near distance the land promised to them through Abraham. A thousand years later, in these same rugged mountains, Jesus would pray and struggle against the devil at the beginning of his ministry. It was no wonder that Jesus quoted Deuteronomy three times during his conversation with Satan (Luke 4:4, 8, 12).

After listening to Moses, the Israelites crossed the river Jordan into the land of Canaan. In the years to come, the people offered to God the first fruits of the ground. Their offerings of the first fruits from the late summer harvest were gifts of gratitude for God's providential care. The people offered those fruits to God, not out of a sense of obligation or through constraint but out of a deep sense of gratitude and joy.

"A wandering Aramean" refers to Jacob, the son of Isaac, who God renamed Israel. However, the description could just as well fit all Israelites who had been rescued from slavery in Egypt and given the amazing gift of a new covenant with God and a new beginning in the Promised Land.

Past and present generations of Israelites become one in this passage from Deuteronomy. The worshiper was called to confess, "Today I declare to the LORD your God that I have come into the land that the LORD swore to our ancestors to give us" (Deuteronomy 26:3). The Israelites who lived years after the people of Israel first entered the Promised Land were just as dependent upon God's saving grace as were those people who had escaped from slavery in Egypt and traveled through the wilderness with Moses.

An interesting part of this tradition was that the worshiping community that offered its first fruits to God was never a closed community. The instructions from Moses further specified that aliens living among them should be invited to share in the harvest bounty. God's grace was so bountiful that there was always enough to share with others. Whenever God's people began to believe that God's bounty was only for them, this story served as a correction. Everyone may be part of God's community.

During these weeks of Lent we, like the ancient Israelites, can also remember anew our dependence upon God. In days past, we may have acted as though our hard work, our money, our possessions, or our military might could save us. However, we owe our lives, our very being, to God's love and grace. Lent gives us the opportunity to recall and celebrate God's blessings. We can rehearse the many different ways that God has blessed us in years past; and with a heart full of gratitude, we can offer our allegiance and praise to God.

Our first clergy appointment together was to seven small congregations in the North Carolina mountains. We, along with our one-year-old daughter, drove north six hours from Atlanta. We traveled into the mountains with all of our worldly belongings piled into a small rental truck, behind which we towed Andy's old VW Beetle. We were inexperienced in ministry. Neither of us had grown up in the mountains. We had no relatives living close by. Indeed, we did not know a single soul in the county to which we were moving. Yet we trusted that God was with us in our travel and in the new home that we would establish. Whatever challenges would come our way, we knew that God and the Christians in those congregations would be there to support us, and so it was. Our four years in the mountains were among the best in our lives.

When has God called you to leave behind places and people you know and to journey to a new land? How has God blessed you on the journey? How can you express your gratitude to God during your Lenten journey?

CONFESS THAT JESUS IS LORD
ROMANS 10:8B-13

Paul, the fanatical rabbi who became an apostle, proclaimed a simple truth that he quoted from the prophet Joel: "Everyone who calls on the name of the Lord shall be saved" (Romans 10:13; Joel 2:32). Paul had never met any of these Christians to whom he wrote; they had discovered Jesus through other preachers. These new followers of Jesus did not live in a physical wilderness. They inhabited the most powerful and extravagant capital in the world, yet imperial Rome was as far from the kingdom of God as east is from west. Those new disciples lived in a spiritual wilderness with no religious landmarks ever seen by Jesus or Paul.

Despite that spiritual distance, Paul believed that those first Christians were part of Jesus' new community. Paul made his affirmation based on his belief that God's gift of salvation through Jesus Christ was extended to all persons who had faith.

Paul wrote his letter to the church in Rome at the end of his third missionary journey to Asia Minor and Greece, around A.D. 57. Paul was staying in Corinth, but he would soon travel to Jerusalem with a financial offering for the needy Jewish Christians. From Jerusalem, Paul hoped to journey westward to Rome and Spain. In fact, Paul would make that journey from Jerusalem to Rome, not as a free man but as a prisoner of the Roman government. He would arrive in Rome, not of his own volition but under Roman guard.

Paul may well have been addressing in his letter to the Romans the tensions between Jewish and Gentile Christians. The Jewish Christians understood themselves as God's covenant people, while the Gentile Christians came to faith outside the traditions of Jewish law. Profound cultural differences may well have been affected by the expulsion of Jews from Rome in the late 40's and their subsequent return when the decree was rescinded after the death of Claudius in A.D. 54. Paul would be encountering a divided congregation of Jewish and Gentile Christians who were uneasy with one another.[1]

According to Paul, none of the Roman Christians had a more privileged position before God. The religious actions of neither the Jewish Christians nor the Gentile Christians made them right with God. There was no pecking order, Paul wrote, "since all have sinned and fall short of the glory of God" (Romans 3:23). All of them were nomads together in the wilderness. The Roman Christians could do or think nothing on their own to receive God's gift of righteousness, yet everyone of them would be saved! Jewish and Gentile Christians were blessed by God. Salvation was a gift from God, not an achievement by human beings.

John Wesley, the father of The United Methodist Church, also struggled to understand that truth of free grace. For the first thirty years of his life, Wesley struggled hard to be a faithful Christian, observing faithfully many religious disciplines; but none of those practices provided for him the assurance of his faith. Then on May 24, 1738, Wesley had a profound religious experience at a Bible study in London while reflecting on Paul's wisdom for the Romans. Wesley described his experience:

> In the evening I went very unwillingly to a society in Aldersgate Street, where a member was reading Luther's preface to the Epistle to the Romans. About a quarter before nine, while the reader was describing the change which God works in the heart through faith in Christ, I felt my heart strangely warmed. I felt I did trust in Christ, Christ alone, for salvation; and an assurance was given me that Jesus Christ had taken away my sins, even mine, and saved me from the law of sin and death.[2]

Sometimes Christians today also have a difficult time accepting God's gift of grace. Sally remembers the altar call at the end of Sunday morning worship service in her home church in Georgia. As a youth, Sally responded to the altar call and walked down the aisle to the front of the church, not once but on numerous occasions. Now there is nothing wrong with altar calls; we all need to be invited to commit our lives to Jesus Christ. The problem for Sally was that she did not trust that God had saved her the first time she walked down the aisle. She thought she needed to prove her devotion to Jesus all over again and to keep striving for worthiness in the eyes of God. Not so, says Paul. God is generous, and "everyone who calls on the name of the Lord shall be saved" (10:13).

An old story relates how a Christian missionary was attempting to translate the New Testament but could not find the right word for "faith." The missionary was searching for a word to express a deep trust in God's power to save. One day, while the translator was working, a native messenger delivered some news and then fell exhausted into a chair. The missionary had a spark of insight. "Explain to me," the missionary asked the messenger, "how it feels to throw yourself into that chair, knowing that the chair will hold you upright." On the chair, the messenger replied with one native word that meant "I trust the chair with my whole weight." That was the word the missionary used for "faith."

That is how we throw ourselves upon God. Through the gift of Jesus Christ, God saves us. We can trust our whole being on that belief.

How do you understand the relationship between your beliefs and actions and the gift of God's salvation in Jesus Christ? How do you experience God's grace?

JESUS IN THE WILDERNESS
LUKE 4:1-13

Picture the scene. The Mount of Temptation, known only through tradition, overlooks the lower Jordan River valley. The mountains are tall, rugged, and barren and stand above the oasis of Jericho, an area rich with water, fig trees, and cattle. Following his baptism by John in the Jordan, Jesus left the fertile valley and journeyed into the mountains for forty days of prayer and reflection. In Native American cultures, such a journey is called a vision quest, a time apart for a young adult to seek a vision from God.

During Jesus' vision quest, he prepared through prayer for his earthly ministry and his death on the cross. Agreeing to God's plan for him was not easy for Jesus. As we read in this Scripture, Jesus was tempted to let go of God's purpose for his life and to accept instead the devil's offers of an easy way out.

The devil came to Jesus after Jesus had abstained from food for several weeks and was hungry, thirsty, and vulnerable. The word for "devil" in Greek is *diabolos*; it means "prone to slander," "a slanderer," or "accusing falsely." The word is also applied to anyone who opposes the will of God. The devil's intention was to separate Jesus from his commitment to his God-given ministry in the world.

Jesus faced three temptations. First, the devil tempted Jesus to end his hunger quickly by commanding a nearby stone to become bread that he could eat. Jesus confessed instead, "One does not live by bread alone" (Luke 4:4).

Second, the devil tempted Jesus by showing him all the kingdoms of the world. Political power was his for the taking, if only Jesus would worship the devil. Still Jesus was faithful and repeated the words of Scripture: "Worship the Lord your God, / and serve only him" (verse 8).

The devil, however, was persistent in his efforts to get Jesus off track. So as a third temptation, he took Jesus to Jerusalem and stood with him on the pinnacle of the Jewish Temple. There he challenged Jesus to jump in order that he might demonstrate how he, the Son of God, would be rescued from death by God's angels. Once again, Jesus stood firm in the face of temptation: "Do not put the Lord your God to the test," Jesus countered.

Confronted by Jesus' faithfulness, the devil left Jesus alone (verses 12-13). All of Jesus' responses came from Moses' message to God's people in Deuteronomy 6:13, 16 and 8:3.

Jesus was tempted to let go of the true self given to him by God. Taking on a false self would separate Jesus from God's love and grace, but the devil tempted Jesus with the promise of glory in the eyes of the world. It seemed so easy. By turning stones into bread, Jesus could be relevant. By accepting the devil's offer to rule the kingdoms of the world, Jesus could be powerful. Finally, by throwing himself off the pinnacle of the Temple into the arms of God's angels, Jesus could be spectacular.

However, Jesus had encountered God during those forty days in the wilderness. He was God's beloved Son; and assured by that truth, Jesus stood firm in the face of the devil's temptations. Instead of choosing the values of the world—popularity, fame, success, and security—Jesus chose to remain faithful to God's calling and to be humble and self-giving.

In the early church, Jesus' forty days in the wilderness became the model of preparation for Easter. The early Christians, and Christians today, strive to experience during Lent some of what Jesus experienced in the days after his baptism. By taking on practices of prayer and self-denial, we as followers of Christ strive to open ourselves to the power of God at work in our lives. We, like Jesus, want to be faithful to our true God-given selves, not to the false selves offered to us by the world.

It can be easy to lose focus on God in the midst of our efforts to keep Lenten disciplines. In the midst of giving up chocolate (like Sally) or taking on exercise routines (like Andy), we find that our focus has shifted from God to self-serving efforts to lose weight. Others of us get up earlier to pray or set aside a day each week to fast; but instead of experiencing renewed closeness to God, we feel self-righteous in light of our friends' less rigorous Lenten practices.

Our disciplines of prayer and self-denial are not for the purpose of winning God's grace or proving to others how holy we are. Instead, Lenten disciplines ideally serve as a means of grace by which we receive that which God offers us. By praying and reading our Bibles every day or by exercising more regularly and giving up certain foods, we open ourselves to God's transforming presence with us.

Every Sunday at Belmont United Methodist Church in Nashville, Tennessee, Bruce Adams placed a beautiful arrangement of roses in the sanctuary. Bruce gave the roses from his rose garden to the glory of God and for the enjoyment of the worshipers. Through much of the year we marveled in the beauty of those roses: deep red, delicate pink, and pale yellow roses to name only a few.

Now God, of course, created Bruce's roses; but God's roses could not have happened apart from Bruce's hard work. When Sally went to visit Bruce, she was likely to find him out among the roses. Bruce spent hours weeding, pruning, watering, fertilizing, and spraying those rose plants. In order for us to enjoy beautiful roses on Sunday morning, though, Bruce had to labor in his rose garden every day. Ultimately, the roses were a gift from God.

Like beautiful roses, strong Christian faith does not just happen. The season of Lent serves as a reminder that if you are to experience the joys and blessings of being disciples of Jesus Christ, there is work for you to do.

God's grace is free, but you are not just saved by grace; you must live by grace. For that reason, place yourself daily in the position to receive God's love and mercy. God wants to change you and transform you into a loving and faithful person; but if you neglect to pray, read your Bible, come to worship, and give your time and money away for the sake of others, you simply will not grow as a Christian. God cannot do God's work in your life if you do not do your work.

In what ways have you been tempted to take on false goals and abandon your God-given purpose? What spiritual disciplines might you practice to bring you closer to the presence of God?

Keep a journal

[1] From *The New Interpreter's Bible*, Volume X (Abingdon Press); pages 406-407.
[2] From *The Works of Wesley*, Volume 18, edited by W. Reginald Ward and Richard P. Heitzenrater (Abingdon, 1988); pages 249-50.

Expect the Promise to Be Fulfilled

Scriptures for Lent:
The Second Sunday
Genesis 15:1-12, 17-18
Philippians 3:17–4:1
Luke 13:31-35

In today's Scriptures, God is the primary actor who forms the new creation; our calling is to hope and trust God to lead us into this new kingdom. In Genesis, God instructed Abram to leave his homeland, promising that he would receive a land flowing with milk and honey. Through God's faithfulness, Abram, whose name was changed to Abraham to signify God's covenant with him, became the father of a people as numerous as the stars in the sky.

Unfortunately, the people of Israel were not always faithful to the covenant God first made with Abraham. Centuries after God's covenant with Abraham, Jesus lamented that Jerusalem had rejected God's covenantal promise of a coming kingdom. In the face of political and religious opposition, Jesus longed to gather, like a protective mother hen, God's people under his wings and re-establish an intimate relationship with his people (Matthew 23:37; Luke 13:34).

It was through Jesus' sacrificial death and resurrection in Jerusalem that God's covenant was re-enacted with the people of God.

About thirty years later, Paul reminded the new Christians in Philippi that they also had become citizens of a new kingdom established through Jesus Christ. No longer were they citizens of imperial Rome or a pagan society; now and forever, they belonged to the kingdom of God (Philippians 3:20).

Today, God is also calling us to be part of God's kingdom. As a follower of Christ and a member of the body of Christ, each of us can embody the love of Christ in our hurting world. Our hands are Jesus' hands, and our heart is Jesus' heart as we participate in the kingdom of God here and now. Even more so, we can look forward with hope to the end of our journey when God in Christ will welcome us into a new creation where there is no pain, suffering, or death.

Even though we now contend with the powers of evil and death, we can all take hope in knowing that we will one day wear crowns, if only we persevere and stand firm in the Lord. As Christians, we give thanks during Lent that "in life, in death, in life beyond death, we are not alone. Thanks be to God."[1]

A COVENANT MADE AND KEPT
GENESIS 15:1-12, 17-18

Approximately four thousand years ago, Abram lived in the town of Haran, in the land of Ur, between the Tigris and Euphrates rivers in the area we now call southern Iraq. When he was seventy-five years old, God came to Abram and told him to leave the rich, fertile land and travel to a new country. At this time, Abram and his wife, Sarai, had no children; but God promised that if Abram would follow, then God would make Abram the father of a great nation.

In response to God's call, Abram gathered his family, flocks, and possessions. He followed the road God set before him. Abram and Sarai journeyed over a thousand miles, northwest up the Euphrates River, west over to Syria, and then down south to the land promised. The travelers fought and won several battles and encountered many obstacles.

Ten years passed. Abram was now eighty-five years old, and Sarai was seventy-five. Yet they had not received the promised child. Surely Abram had doubts: "How am I to know that I shall possess the promises God made to me?" This nomadic family had abandoned the materialism of the Chaldeans, escaped the Babylonian way of life, and undertaken a long journey. Had not the time arrived for proof of God's faithfulness? It is at this point that we pick up the story.

Each of us, like Abram, has dreams, which we hope are God-given. We yearn to live full lives. We long for financial stability. We want our parents to age gracefully. We desire to be free from pain and hurt. We look forward to abundant lives for our children. We dream that people will be fed and that peace will reign. How does God respond to these dreams? Sometimes we fail, people we love die, illness strikes, our children disappoint us, and the world falls into chaos. All of us have had dreams crushed, hopes put down, and expectations left unmet. We ask, "Where are you taking us God?"

As for Abram, God came to him in a vision and told him not to be afraid. Because Abram had been faithful, he would receive everything God promised. God told Abram to go outside and count the stars in the sky (Genesis 15:5). Then God declared that the descendants of Abram would be as countless as the stars. In addition, Abram's people would inherit land that spread from the Nile River to the Euphrates River (verse 18). First, however, a child would be born.

The two of us once took an anniversary vacation to south Florida. On a clear May night, we stood in the Everglades National Park. There were no human-made lights within dozens of miles to brighten the night sky. As we looked up, we saw the heavens as we had never seen them before. The sky was bright with stars so plentiful that we could not even begin to count even one small quadrant of the sky. Humbled by the power of God's creation, we caught a glimpse of the promise God made to Abram.

On more than one occasion in the Book of Genesis, God made covenant with God's chosen people. A covenant is an oath by two parties, in which each promises to do something for the other. In God's covenant with Abram, God dealt first (verses 1-6) with the promise of Abram's descendants.

The second part of this Scripture (verses 7-12) describes the covenant's contents and the ritual for its enactment. Here, as elsewhere, the initiative was God's. Offered without precondition, the covenant nevertheless required a response. Would Abram and his heirs have faith in God's promise? Even more significantly, would Abram and his heirs remain faithful to the God who initiated the covenant in the first place?

The ritual described was intense and impressive. God cut a covenant with Abraham, an ancient practice where participants in a covenant oath passed through dismembered parts of an animal. The sacrifice offered affirmed the covenant. God assured Abram that the covenant would be fulfilled. The promise of an heir was trustworthy. "Do not be afraid, Abram, I am your shield; your reward will be very great" (verse 1). Ultimately, God issued Abram a challenge and a command almost impossible to refuse.

The author of the New Testament book Hebrews described suc-cinctly the audacious faith of Abram, who later would receive a fuller name: "By faith Abraham obeyed when he was called to set out for a place that he was to receive as an inheritance; and he set out, not knowing where he was going" (Hebrews 11:8). So shall we continue our own journeys into Lent.

Psalm 27, the additional Scripture for this second Sunday of Lent, is a confident and triumphant expression of faith. It is traditionally attributed to David, the shepherd king of Israel and one of Abraham's heirs. The psalm begins by declaring to the world, "The LORD is my light and my salvation; / whom shall I fear? / The LORD is the stronghold of my life; / of whom shall I be afraid" (Psalm 27:1). Throughout David's life, he faced daunting foes: the giant Goliath, King Saul, enemy armies, and even his own passions for sexual conquest and political power. In that vein, whether it was Abraham journeying to a new land or Paul writing letters in prison or Jesus looking toward his death in Jerusalem, each could say, "Wait for the LORD; / be strong, and let your heart take courage; / wait for the LORD!" (Psalm 27:14).

How do you claim God's promises today? What do you expect of God? What does God expect of you? ??? Worship praise read the scriptures

LIVE ACCORDING TO CHRIST
PHILIPPIANS 3:17–4:1

Paul wrote the letter to the church at Philippi from prison. He reassures them at the beginning: "I know that through your prayers and the help of the Spirit of Jesus Christ this will turn out for my deliverance" (Philippians 1:19). He also commended Epaphroditus to them (2:25-30) and expressed his gratitude for the gift the church sent him (4:18). The overriding tone of the letter is one of encouragement.

Paul loved the people of Philippi. The town was a Roman settlement on the northeast coast of Greece. Philippi, named after Philip the Second, the father of Alexander the Great, was the major gateway from Asia Minor (modern-day Turkey) into northern Greece and from there into Europe. The heart of the city was located several miles inland from the bustling seaport.

It was in Philippi that Paul baptized Lydia, cured a woman who had been exploited for her fortune-telling skills, and ended up in jail with his colleague Silas for threatening the major industry of making idols. Being in jail did not dampen Paul's faith; and through prayers and songs, the walls of the jail fell down and the jailer and his family were converted (Acts 16). Paul often spoke of joy in his letter to the Philippians. He was joyous that he and the Christians of Philippi had been partners in ministry.

Because Philippi was a Roman imperial city, it held equal status with the Roman cities of Italy. For that reason, the residents of Philippi were blessed to be free from imperial taxes. Some of the Philippian Christians were citizens of Rome as Paul was. Others were Greek, while still others were slaves and had no citizenship at all. However, Paul reminded all the Christians at Philippi that their citizenship was ultimately not of this world but of God's kingdom.

Understandably, Paul's affirmation of a new kingdom was incendiary and politically threatening. For five hundred years, the Roman Empire had been a republic, ruled over by a senate of diverse persons with differing perspectives. Some democratic checks and balances existed; but in the generation before the birth of Paul, the Roman general Octavian seized control of Rome's military, political, and religious structures.

Octavian was given the title Augustus, which means "revered one"; and to this title, he added the Latin word for king, *Caesar*. In reverence to Caesar Augustus, temples were built throughout the Empire and an imperial cult spread to cities such as Philippi. At first, the Romans did not insist on worship of the king; but strong cultural pressures soon demanded such adoration.

Needless to say, Paul and other Christians existed in uneasy tension with and the possibility of real persecution from the Empire. Instead of Caesar, absolute allegiance belonged to God; and such allegiance required a brand new set of ethical behaviors. Paul suggested to the Philippians that as citizens of God's kingdom they should be like him. At first glance, such a statement by Paul seems rather egotistical, even arrogant. Yes, Paul clearly had a good self image when he called himself a Pharisee of Pharisees; but similarly, all of us realize the importance of good role models: parents for their children, teachers for their students, and elderly adults for new generations. However, Paul's self-confidence was not based on his natural abilities, but in God. Paul boldly made other audacious statements:

"All things work together for good for those who love God." Romans 8:28
"[Nothing] will be able to separate us from the love of God." Romans 8:39
"You are the body of Christ." 1 Corinthians 12:27
"Love never ends." 1 Corinthians 13:8

Paul was bold because he was confident in the promises of Jesus Christ. He trusted not in his own abilities but in Christ's power at work through him. Citizens of the world, including the residents of the Roman town of Philippi, were tempted daily to give in to bodily appetites and to be self-indulgent. Paul urged the Philippians to let go of their worldly behaviors and to trust instead in Christ's vision for the new kingdom.

Living as citizens of the world would lead only to destruction; but living as citizens of Christ's kingdom, the Philippians would experience never-ending communion with God. Jesus himself was the model for Kingdom living.

Let us describe just one aspect of this new Kingdom lifestyle. Paul spoke of "humiliation" (Philippians 3:21), which he himself experienced when he was beaten many times, stoned until he almost died, and shipwrecked twice. However, because Jesus had been humiliated before him, Paul continued to preach the gospel of Jesus Christ. During the upcoming Holy Week, we too will remember that Jesus experienced humiliation through his arrest, torture, suffering, and death.

We, too, are called to model ourselves after Jesus. We are offered another way of life rather than the way of yielding to the standards and temptations of our world. Like the church at Philippi, we are citizens of God's kingdom and are called to live and participate in this kingdom.

In this call we may need to determine what our own humiliation looks like; then we may well discover the same joy that Paul experienced. Perhaps it is as simple as giving up a dinner at a restaurant so that we may volunteer instead at the local homeless shelter. Maybe it is as difficult as taking a pay cut or turning down a promotion so that other workers will not lose their jobs. As we choose according to God's way revealed in Jesus Christ, like Paul, we will discover that Christ "will transform the body of our humiliation that it may be conformed to the body of his glory" (verse 21).

How can you live as a citizen of the kingdom of God, especially in this Lenten season? What ways of the world must you reject? What new behaviors can you take on in order that you might become more like Christ?

GATHERING THE BROOD
LUKE 13:31-35

Jesus' prayer over Jerusalem stands as one of the most poignant passages in the Bible. The Scripture begins with a warning to Jesus. Herod, son of the ruler who slaughtered the children in Bethlehem at Jesus' birth, had heard stories about Jesus. This Herod was just as ruthless as his father and had shown no reluctance in beheading John the Baptist. Now Herod had his sights on the Galilean prophet Jesus. Some Pharisees, who had aligned themselves with Jesus, brought to Jesus rumors that Herod meant to kill him. Jesus listened to the threats and then answered, "Go and tell that fox for me, 'Listen, I am casting out demons and performing cures today and tomorrow, and on the third day I finish my work'" (Luke 13:32).

Jesus, who compared himself to a hen who gathers her brood under her wings, would not be intimidated by Herod; his threats did not scare Jesus. Jesus knew that nothing and no one could stop God's work of love through him. His destiny was in God's hands. No one, not even Herod, could lay hands on him until the God-given time. The final showdown would be on God's terms and in Jerusalem. On Good Friday, when Jesus finally stood before Herod face to face, he refused to back down.

No doubt Jesus' disciples were frightened by the Pharisees' warnings. How could Jesus stand up to the overpowering strength of the religious establishment and the Roman government? The religious and political leaders of Galilee and Judea had been working against Jesus ever since he first spoke with authority in the synagogue in his hometown of Nazareth. Jesus was not worried; but the disciples must have wondered, *Could Jesus overcome the anger of the Pharisees and the devious plots of the chief priests and scribes?*

It was Jesus who shifted the focus from Herod's threats to the city of Jerusalem and its people. Jesus was no stranger to Jerusalem, the city of peace. He was born in the shadow of this great capital (Bethlehem was just eight miles south) and had been honored in the Temple for his knowledge when he was only twelve years old. Jerusalem was the religious and political center of the nation, and all of Jesus' major adversaries lived within the city's walls. In Jerusalem, Jesus would soon be celebrated with palm branches and hosannas; and right outside Jerusalem's walls, Jesus would be hanged on a cross.

The traditional site for Jesus' lament over Jerusalem is a spot on the Mount of Olives, just east of the city. Looking across the Kidron Valley, Jesus mourned that the people of Jerusalem had rejected his offer of a new kingdom even as they had rejected the offers from God's prophets in years past. Jesus longed to bring all of God's chosen people into his arms, but the people had turned away from God's love. Now it was too late. Jesus would soon travel into Jerusalem and be executed.

Others before Jesus had looked upon Jerusalem from the same

spot on the Mount of Olives. The Assyrians saw a fortress to conquer, the Babylonians gazed on a city to plunder, and the Romans discovered a people to control. Jesus looked upon the city built on Mount Zion and beheld a community of people to be loved and protected.

At the end of this Scripture, Jesus turned his back on Jerusalem with this prophetic statement: "You will not see me until the time comes when you say, 'Blessed is the one who comes in the name of the Lord'"(verse 35). These words foreshadow the triumphal entry into Jerusalem and echo words from Psalm 118:26 that were sung by pilgrims who entered Jerusalem.[2]

Jesus mourned when he thought about the people of Jerusalem; and so, too, do we mourn when we think about our own lives and communities. The truth is that none of us has used our God-given talents and abilities to their full potential. All of us have disappointed our families, our churches, our home communities, our global community, and ourselves.

Too often, we have given in to anxieties about the future and focused on security for ourselves alone. We have met only minimal expectations of work colleagues and family members. We have ignored the needs of the people around us while isolating ourselves in our homes to watch television or surf the Internet.

When Andy was a freshman in college, he was taught by one of the same professors who taught his father twenty-five years earlier. Professor Abernathy and Andy's father had developed a strong pro-

fessional and personal friendship over the years. Andy made a B+ on his first test in Dr. Abernathy's class. Andy had reason to be pleased; that B+ was the best grade in the class. Yet the only comment on his paper was, "You can do better."

At first, Andy was angry. Should not the best paper be an A? Was he being compared unjustly to his father? Dr. Abernathy invited Andy to his office. There this experienced professor shared that he had great expectations for Andy and would not let him settle for anything other than his best. Andy took the challenge, and for the next few years learned much from Dr. Abernathy.

Throughout the Bible, God's people have accepted God's challenge to become more. Abram left his home and journeyed to a land he had never seen. Paul departed Jerusalem and traveled the Roman world at great danger to himself. Simon, Andrew, James, and John left their fishing boats to follow Jesus. Mary sat at Jesus' feet and listened to his teachings. Zacchaeus climbed down from the sycamore tree and gave half of his money to the poor. Often we settle for less than what God can give us; but might we, like those who have gone before us, find courage to become more through our confidence in God's love?

Jesus' image of the mother hen, gathering her brood under her wings, is a powerful one. When a fox attacks, when rain falls, or when cold air rushes in, all good mothers become single-mindedly protective of their children. When someone unjustly criticizes our daughters, watch out for Sally.

How much more so is that true with God. When temptation threatens us, when our crises hit, when our faith grows cold, God surrounds us with wings of love and protection and gives us courage to keep going.

We all have had days when we wondered if we were up to the challenge of following Jesus. Our efforts seem so small compared to the forces of evil and violence in our communities and around the world. Even so, we can find courage to keep striving for the end of poverty, hunger, war, and oppression by remembering Jesus' refusal to be intimidated by that fox Herod.

In Lent, the cross of Christ looms before us; but we do not have to fear the journey to the cross. We can trust instead in God's love, which is powerful enough to empty the tomb. God's love can handle any challenge we face. Not even death will pull us away from shelter under the wings of our loving God.

When have you felt the need to make a difference in a situation in your community? How does Jesus' courage offer hope for what you might do to make a difference?

---

[1]From "A Statement of Faith of The United Church of Canada" in *The United Methodist Hymnal*, 883.
[2]From *The New Interpreter's Bible*, Volume IX; page 282.

Repent and Believe

Scriptures for Lent:
The Third Sunday
Isaiah 55:1-9
1 Corinthians 10:1-13
Luke 13:1-9

What is expected of God's people as we continue our journey toward Jerusalem, Christ's Passion, and the Resurrection? The call to repentance is one that many people put off until it is too late to respond to God's call.

When are we going to die? In fifty years? in twenty years? in ten years? or perhaps even today? None of us knows the hour of our death. We do not know how long we have to live, yet most of us act as though we have unlimited time. Wrongly believing that we will live forever, we postpone important decisions about our spiritual, emotional, intellectual, and physical well-being; but we do not have all the time in the world. None of us even has a guarantee that we will be alive tomorrow. If we are going to make changes in our lives, we must start making them today.

In all of today's Scripture passages, God offers us life. Isaiah 55:1-9 calls the wicked to "forsake their way, and the unrighteous their thoughts; let them return to the LORD" (Isaiah 55:7). Fortunately, the cleansing power of God is more life-giving than can be imagined. In 1 Corinthinans 10:13, Paul warns the Corinthians against following the wayward actions of the people of God in the wilderness and the general pagan culture in Corinth. In Luke 13:1-9, Jesus reminds his disciples that repentance precedes faithfulness. Commenting on two local tragedies in Jerusalem, Jesus called his disciples to bear fruit worthy of his message or face certain destruction.

God has high expectations of a holy people. This Sunday in Lent offers a wonderful opportunity to let go of sin and to embrace that which brings life, healing, and meaning. Today and throughout Lent, we have the opportunity to seize the moment and choose the life God offers. We can trust God to forgive us and to help us turn our lives around.

HUNGRY AND THIRSTY FOR GOD
ISAIAH 55:1-9

Isaiah 55 is Sally's favorite passage in the Bible. It was the text on the first Sunday she preached following graduation from seminary, and she has eagerly preached from this passage many times in the years since then. The passage speaks powerfully of the hunger and thirst we all have for a relationship with God. Centuries ago, Saint Augustine, a follower of Jesus from North Africa, prayed fervently to God:

You called and cried out loud and shattered my deafness.

You were radiant and resplendent, you put to flight my blindness.

You were fragrant, and I drew in my breath and now pant after you.

I tasted you, and I feel but hunger and thirst for you.

You touched me, and I am set on fire to attain the peace which is yours.

Augustine, *Confessions*, 10.27

We also are hungry and thirsty for God. Unfortunately, we tend to forget that God is ever ready to feed us and to quench our thirsts.

The Israelites also had the tendency to forget God's love and care. During one period of Israel's history, the people trusted not in God for security but in foreign alliances and military might. Of course, when Nebuchadnezzar and the Babylonians invaded Israel, plundered the land, and carted the people off to exile in Babylon, the Israelites were given a harsh reminder that God alone can be trusted.

The years spent in Babylon were hard ones. The people longed for the homes they had left behind.

They cried, "By the rivers of Babylon— / there we sat down and there we wept / when we remembered Zion" (Psalm 137:1). The good news is that just as God had heard the cries of the people when they were slaves in Egypt, God heard their cries when they were exiles in Babylon. This passage from Isaiah was written with the expectation that the people would soon return home to Jerusalem.

The prophet shared with the people a beautiful vision of what home would look like: "For you shall go out in joy, and be led back in peace; the mountains and the hills before you shall burst into song, and all the trees of the field shall clap their hands" (Isaiah 55:12).

The Israelites had a new opportunity to go home to God. Isaiah 55 reminds them not to forget the lessons they had learned: "Why do you spend your money for that which is not bread, / and labor for that which does not satisfy?" (verse 2). The Scripture reminds the people of their covenant relationship with God and calls them to seek and call upon God who remains near to them (verse 6).

Our journeys through Lent have as their destination a renewed and life-giving relationship with God. Can you remember an occasion when through God's grace you accepted the gift of "wine and milk without money and without price"? (verse 1). Perhaps you dragged yourself out of bed earlier than usual to pray and read the Bible and discovered again the grandeur of God's world as you watched the rising of the sun. Or maybe you decided against buying that colorful purse or fancy gadget and found deep satisfaction instead in writing a generous check to a local food pantry. Or instead of putting in a few extra hours at work on your day off, perhaps you drove to a nearby nursing home to visit lonely residents and experienced the healing of your own loneliness.

On more than one occasion, we all have learned that loving and serving God is the source of nourishing food and thirst-quenching drink. Why then do we continue to neglect eating "what is good" and delighting ourselves in "rich food" and instead "spend our money for that which is not bread" and "labor for that which does not satisfy"? (verse 2).

A couple of years ago, Sally underwent a lumpectomy and radiation for breast cancer. She is now doing fine and is grateful for the support she had during her illness from a loving God and faithful friends and family. What she realized during the radiation treatments was that she had taken her life for granted. It was as though she thought she would live forever. Sally assumed that someday there would always be time to put first things first; but that time was today, not tomorrow.

Sally's experience is not unique. Many of us have had similar experiences when we have come face to face with the truth that life is precious. Today is the only time we have to focus on what counts in our lives. That challenging invitation from God comes through loud and clear in today's Scripture from the prophet Isaiah.

Lent can be the ideal time for assessing our spiritual health. We can begin by looking for danger signs. If we believe that we are indispensable in our jobs or in our local churches, then that is a sign that we are "spending our money for that which is not bread."

Think about it. When any of us take on too many responsibilities at church or feel guilty about letting someone else teach Sunday school or lead a mission work team, then we have put our trust in ourselves, not in God. At the other extreme, we are also "laboring for that which is not bread" when we have become so busy with family, recreational, or sports activities that we no longer have time to offer our talents for God and our local church community.

Either way, we have lost our focus on God and God's gift of meaningful and satisfying life. Isaiah calls all of us to come to God and listen so that we might live (verse 3).

When have you experienced God's gift of life? In what ways is God inviting you to "come, buy, and eat" during this Lenten season?

DO NOT FALL
1 CORINTHIANS 10:1-13

Corinth was a major trading capital of Greece, a seaport linking the Aegean Sea to the east and the Adriatic Sea to the west. During the time of Paul, the city was the center of commerce between Rome and the Asian provinces and was larger, more prosperous, and more influential than Athens. It was also a city of cultural and religious diversity. Syrians, Phoenicians, Egyptians, Greeks, Romans, Jews, and Asians all resided in Corinth. Most of the residents therefore were not Jewish but were worshipers of a variety of gods. The ancient historian Pausanias recorded that there was "a temple for all the gods" in Corinth.

Corinth also had a reputation as one of the most corrupt and disorderly cities of the Empire. Alciphron, another ancient author, wrote that the Corinthians were "without grace and not the least convivial."[1]

Paul stayed in Corinth a year and a half, during which time he introduced the Corinthians to Jesus and became the founding pastor of a new Christian community. Paul would visit the town on two other occasions. In Corinth, Paul took on a tent-making job in the shop of Aquila and Priscilla, who became lifelong friends. Perhaps the shop was right off the square, under the shadow of the temples to Greek gods.

Athletes and games were highly valued in the culture of Corinth as they are in our culture. The biennial Isthmian games were held near Corinth and had occurred within a year of Paul's first letter.[2] Imagine how those Greek games would have been the talk of the town—not so different from the heightened publicity in the months before the modern-day Summer and Winter Olympics.

Immediately before the events in 1 Corinthians 9:24-27, Paul uses athletic images from these famous games in order to urge the people to be persistent, faithful, and steadfast in their Christian pilgrimage. Paul wanted them to persevere no matter what challenges and obstacles society threw at them.

As new Christians, the Corinthians were called to a brand new way of relating to one another. No longer, for example, could the rich church members think of themselves as better than the poor church members. In the body of Christ, each member is important. There is room—and food—for each member at the Lord's Table (11:17-33).

The Corinthians faced the specific challenge every day of where to buy the food they would eat. Most of the animals slaughtered were first offered to one or another of the gods. While a small piece of fat would be burnt on an altar to a god, the rest of the food would be sold in the market; but as Paul reminded the Corinthians, these gods were not real so, theoretically, Christians could eat food offered to idols (8:1-13). However, the Corinthian Christians no longer had to worry only about themselves. If they offended Christians weak in their faith by eating food offered to idols, then by all means they should refuse that food (8:13). Concern for one another was more important than a full plate of food.

In Chapter 10, Paul warns the Corinthian Christians not to take their faith for granted. The Israelites before them had also received God's gift of life when they were led out of slavery in Egypt; but receiving that gift did not keep some of the Israelites from giving in to temptation and letting go of their dependence on God. Paul cautioned the Corinthians that they were also in danger of losing the life they had received through Jesus Christ. Even as Christians, they were susceptible to corruption. Unless they were careful, they, like their ancestors, would become indulgent, self-willed, and overconfident.

Paul challenged his friends to eat only the food that would satisfy them forever. He evoked memories of the Exodus and the manna that God provided to Moses and the liberated Israelites in the Sinai wilderness as well as the water God provided from a rock. The people of Israel had sometimes longed for the security of Egypt and its pots of food, but God alone was steadfast and sure. If the people would abstain from pagan practices, Paul argued, "God is faithful, and he will not let you be tested beyond your strength, but with the testing he will also provide the way out so that you may be able to endure it" (verse 13).

Paul's letter reminds us that our own spiritual disciplines can be practices to keep us focused on love and service to God. As the people of Israel passed through the waters of the sea from slavery to freedom, the Christians passed from death to life through the waters of baptism. In baptism, the early Christians rejected all loyalty to Satan and pledged their allegiance to God. Baptism holds the same significance for us today.

Similarly, the sacrament of Holy Communion can offer us, as it did the Corinthian Christians, the spiritual nourishment we need.

Instead of settling for food offered to idols, the blood of animals and their flesh, the Corinthian Christians gathered around the Lord's Table to share in the blood and body of Jesus Christ. When we, too, drink from the cup of salvation and eat the bread of life, we are reminded that God provides food that is satisfying and sufficient. With the bread and drink God provides, we will never hunger again. If there is any season to celebrate weekly Holy Communion, Lent is that season.

In Lent, we are tempted over and over again to forget our spiritual disciplines and to yield instead to the priorities and values of our culture. At the beginning of Lent, we are eager to take on disciplines such as prayer, fasting, and sacrificial giving in order to stay focused on our journey with Jesus to the cross. As the weeks of Lent go by, however, we are all tempted to minimize the importance of our spiritual disciplines.

Today, we have the choice of yielding to the culture around us, dabbling in false idols, or eating the food that will not nourish us. When we do so, we miss what Paul experienced as a meaningful, fulfilling, and everlasting life. Paul reminds us as he reminded the church at Corinth that God is faithful. We have what we need to live God's way revealed in Jesus Christ.

What are the idols in your life or in our culture that tempt you from the way of life shown through Jesus Christ?

UNFRUITFUL TREES
LUKE 13:1-9

The Gospel passage today presents a critical message for Lent: Repent and turn toward God while time remains. The Scripture begins with a discussion about justice and then shifts to the need for human beings to be responsible.

Jesus was speaking to a self-satisfied crowd of people. The crowd that had gathered to listen to Jesus could easily see other people's sins and failures. These people were eager to gossip about two tragedies that had recently occurred within Jerusalem. First, Pilate, the Roman leader in Jerusalem, had killed some Jews from Galilee. This is the same Pontius Pilate who would condemn Jesus to crucifixion on Good Friday. As the Galileans were offering their sacrifices to God in the Temple, a peaceful, worshipful act, Pilate sent Roman soldiers to kill them, thus mingling their blood with their sacrifices. What bad things, the crowd asked Jesus, had the Galileans done to bring on their deaths?

What about the eighteen people who had been crushed to death when the Tower of Siloam in Jerusalem collapsed on them? What did those victims do, the crowd asked Jesus, to deserve such an awful death as that? A parallel in our day and time might be a deadly hurricane or an earthquake. What, might we ask, did the people who died do to deserve such a tragic and untimely end? Or consider the thousands who were killed through the actions of terrorists on September 11. What did our nation do to deserve such horrible pain and loss?

"Not anything," Jesus answered. According to Jesus, there was no connection between the suffering of those people and their failures. He broke the connection between sin and punishment. He reminded the crowd that suffering is not always the result of sin, but then Jesus turned his focus onto the crowd itself. This crowd of people, so busy talking about others, had failed to see their own failures. "Unless you repent," Jesus told them, "you will all perish just as they did" (Luke 13:5).

To guarantee that the people understood what he was saying, Jesus told them the story of the unfruitful fig tree. A landowner could find no figs on one of his fig trees, even though the soil was good and the location appropriate. Let us paraphrase the conversation between the landowner and his gardener. The owner began, "Look at this tree! For three years I have come looking for tasty figs, and still I find not one. Cut the tree down! Why should an unfruitful fig tree take up precious space and labor?" The gardener countered to the landowner, "Wait. What if we give the fig tree one more year to produce fruit? I will dig around the tree and fertilize it. Next year, if the tree is still barren, then I will cut it down myself."

In this parable, God is the landowner, Jesus is the gardener, and we are the tree. The parable is clear and unambiguous. Even though the unfruitful tree bears no fruit, the gardener wishes to nurture it and give it every opportunity possible to grow. However, during this reprieve, Jesus holds a mirror in front of us and asks, "What do you see?" Do we see a person whose words, actions, and attitudes are faithful to the gospel; or do we see a person living far from the will of God? Jesus adds, "Unless you repent, you will perish."

The crowd gathered around Jesus could not have missed his word of judgment. God loved them; but unless they started bearing fruit, they, like the fig tree, might be cut down. Unless they started living like God's people, their future would be short.

Jesus' story of judgment is also a story of grace. God's judgment was coming, but not yet. The people still had time to turn around, to start moving in the right direction. The fig tree was given a one-year reprieve. Likewise, the people still had time to repent and change their lives.

Jesus' story of the unfruitful fig tree speaks directly to us. Have we born fruit worthy of all that God has invested in us? Have we used our time, talents, and resources for the sake of the Kingdom? Sometimes we are like that gossiping crowd. We read in the papers or see on television or find on the Internet reports of stupid, ignorant people getting exactly what they deserve. If you jump off a roof onto a trampoline, can anything good happen? Most of us reading this resource are surely better than they.

Jesus, however, does not let us off that easily. Salvation is a free gift. We do not have to do anything to win God's gift of everlasting love, but we do have to receive that gift; and once we receive that gift of love, we must allow God's love to change our lives. If we do not change, if we do not produce good fruit, then something is wrong. We must repent, get back on track, and ask God to take charge of our lives all over again.

Alfred Nobel was a Swedish chemist who helped developed effective explosives for mining and construction. Later, that same technology was used in warfare. One night Nobel's brother died in a car accident, but the newspapers got the report mixed up and reported that Nobel was the one who had died. In his obituary, Nobel was remembered as the world's dynamite king. The newspaper reported that Nobel had made an incredible fortune by developing explosives for mass destruction.

Nobel read his obituary and was disturbed by the way in which his life had been interpreted to the world. For Nobel, the good news was that he still had time to turn his life around. Nobel set up a series of international awards to be given to people who made positive contributions to humankind. Today we know those awards as the Nobel Prizes, one of which is the Nobel Peace Prize.[3]

Repentance can be the beginning of a renewed relationship with God. *Repent* literally means "turn around." Repentance asks us to adopt a completely new orientation that influences every aspect of life, and such repentance leads to a life that is more likely to be fruitful.

What do you need to do to be more fruitful as you seek to love and serve God and your neighbor? What difference would repentance, or "turning around" to God's ways, make in your relationship with God and with your neighbor?

[1] From *The New Interpreter's Bible,* Volume X; pages 773-75.

[2] From *The New Interpreter's Study Bible* (Abingdon Press, 2003); page 2049.

[3] From "The Worst and the Brightest," by Frederic Golden in *Time* magazine (October 16, 2000).

Forgiveness is a discipline

Be Reconciled With God

Scriptures for Lent: The Fourth Sunday

Joshua 5:9-12

2 Corinthians 5:16-21

Luke 15:1-3, 11b-32

We are nearing the events of Holy Week. God in Christ has led us to this point in our journey. This week we are asked to be reconciled anew with our God, but who can enter the kingdom of God? Who has the ability needed to live as a faithful disciple?

The Scriptures for this Sunday remind us that God welcomes us home, not on the basis of our achievements but because of God's love. Traditionally, the proclamation of God's love on the fourth Sunday in Lent has served as a refreshing oasis in the disciplined Lenten journey. Receive this fourth set of Scriptures as a necessary resting place in your vigorous journey toward Jerusalem and God's reign.

Forgiveness, for us and for those who sin against us, is an underlying theme of the day. We are presented a fresh start because of God's willingness to take away our disgrace and sin. This is a day to adopt the spiritual discipline of accepting God's forgiveness and forgiving ourselves and others as a way of opening ourselves to being even more deeply reconciled to God. In doing so, we will discover that God has broken down the walls of hostility that separate us from God and one another.

All of today's Scriptures speak loudly of the new life being offered to us by our loving God. Joshua recalled God's love for the people Israel and the first Passover celebrations in the land flowing with milk and honey. Just as God had fed the Israelites manna in the wilderness, so now was God caring for the people in their new home in Canaan. Are we ready to celebrate at the banquet that God has also prepared for us?

According to Paul, we Christians have received the power of the cross and the Resurrection and are a new creation. Thanks to the transforming work of Christ, we are leaving the old behind and becoming a more holy people. Can we celebrate God's mighty acts of salvation in our lives?

From Jesus, we hear the story of the wayward son who was welcomed home by a father whose love was boundless. The father also invited to his party the stay-at-home brother who was jealous of the father's generous love. Similarly, God welcomes all of us to the homecoming feast. Will we accept the invitation?

BEGINNING A NEW JOURNEY
JOSHUA 5:9-12

In the opening chapters of the Book of Joshua, the people of Israel ended one journey and began a new one. Moses had died. Under Joshua's guidance, the people traveled from the far side of the Jordan River, across a dry riverbed, into the land God promised to Abraham. The city of Jericho stood high above them, but the people had confidence that with God's help the city would fall. To renew their covenant with God, Joshua led a ceremony of circumcision of all the men. This ancient act of covenant, a serious sign of commitment, recalled God's promise to Abraham. One part of the people's heritage was reclaimed.

As a sign of this new chapter in their story, the people of God turned the page on their lives in the wilderness and made a fresh start in the Promised Land. It was the end of nomadic wanderings and the beginning of a more settled, agricultural life. No more would manna appear on the ground like dew each morning. From now on, the people would plant and sow their own crops.

At Gilgal, a place name that simply means "rolled away," Joshua presided over the Passover meal. We do not know all the courses served or all the foods eaten, but the meal may have included roasted lamb (remembering the paschal lamb whose blood marked the Jewish homes on the night when death passed over their houses in Egypt), bitter herbs (remembering their suffering in slavery), and unleavened bread (remembering how quickly they had to leave Egypt). For the next three thousand years, and continuing today, the Jewish people would celebrate this meal of remembrance and promise.

Some years ago, Andy and our daughter Sarah were invited to share in the Passover meal at Temple Israel in Charlotte. Rabbi Murray Ezring invited them to sit at his family's table during a community celebration of the holy meal. Between courses of exceptional food and wine, the rabbi, the cantor (song leader), and members of the congregation told the story of the night that for Jews is different from every other night. They ate, drank, read, sang, and laughed throughout the evening. This biblical tradition remains alive and well across our planet.

Christians have their own traditional gatherings that call to mind God's ongoing faithfulness to the Christian community. In the North Carolina mountains, the people of Jonas Ridge celebrate homecoming each year on the second Sunday in July. On top of a high ridge in the Appalachian Mountains, under the shadow of Grandfather Mountain, two small congregations, one United Methodist and the other Baptist, share homecoming celebrations.

Families from far and near gather. People decorate gravestones in the common cemetery. Older adults tell younger children the family stories. After a time of worship, everyone shares in a covered-dish lunch with tables groaning under the weight of fried chicken, country ham, fresh vegetables, biscuits, and desserts of every kind. No one remembers how long homecoming on Jonas Ridge has been celebrated, but its traditions form new generations today.

The Scripture from Joshua can prepare us for the events in Holy Week, even as it reminds us of the continuing presence of God in our lives. It was during the Feast of Unleavened Bread that Jesus shared a meal with his disciples in the upper room. After washing the feet of his disciples, Jesus re-interpreted that meal of remembrance into a meal of new life. The unleavened bread became a sign of his body and the fruit of the vine a sign of his blood. Remembering the Exodus, Jesus looked ahead to a dramatically new liberation from death and the promise of the resurrected life.

As we read Joshua, we might recall the meaning of our baptism. The people of Israel crossed through the waters of the Jordan on dry land, possibly near the location where John baptized Jesus a thousand years later. Just as the people of Israel entered the land promised to them, once they had made their way through the river, so too do Christians today enter into a new relationship with God when they pass through the waters of baptism. Our baptism issues us into the very kingdom of God.

Joshua led the people in religious rituals that marked them as a people reconciled to God and ready to receive the blessings of God in the Promised Land. They remembered and celebrated their journey through the wilderness, a journey fraught with disobedience yet blessed by God's continuing presence and power. The chosen people were ready to remember, celebrate, and accept God's gift of the Promised Land. They had been reshaped and reconciled to God.

Psalm 32, the lectionary psalm for this fourth Sunday in Lent, is an ideal response to the passage from Joshua. It celebrates God's forgiveness and reconciliation. This psalm, which may have been sung during a time of confession in the Temple in Jerusalem, says, "I acknowledged my sin to you, and I did not hide my iniquity. . . . Be glad in the LORD and rejoice" (Psalm 32:5, 11).

We, too, offer our confessions in confidence to God who "forgave the guilt of [our] sin" (Psalm 32:5). To be holy is not to be without sin. Instead, being holy is recognizing God's cleansing power in our lives. Thanks to God we can experience the joy of forgiveness and reconciliation.

Where are you in your journey this week? Are you leaving behind an old country for a new one? Are you leaving behind one lifestyle for another? What meals have sustained you on your journey?

A NEW CREATION
2 CORINTHIANS 5:16-21

In the midst of a city known for its corruption, Paul painted a vision of a new creation full of peace and reconciliation for individual Christians and for all of society. In Paul's day, Corinth was the capital and commercial center of Greece. The sea routes cut east and west through Corinth; the roads ran north and south. Because of its natural geographical location, Corinth served as the commercial crossroads of the Empire.

Separated by just three miles of dry land, one of Corinth's bays faced east to the Aegean Sea and ultimately Rome. The other bay faced west to the Adriatic Sea and the Roman Empire in Asia Minor and the Middle East. Easily traversed roads led north from Corinth to major cities in Asia Minor. Just a hundred years earlier, Julius Caesar had rebuilt the town as a Roman colony; and Caesar Augustus had made it the capital of Greece.

Corinth was recognized as more than the commercial center of the region. In response to the loose lifestyles of the Corinthians, the Greeks developed the word "to corinthianize," which meant "to make a place of vice." In Corinth, every vice associated with port cities ran rampant. Economic corruption prevailed; and temples had been built in Corinth for the many, different religions of the Empire.

Paul, however, had another vision for his Christian friends and that city. Paul saw the world through a new set of lenses in which every division was set aside and every sin overcome. Paul's vision had its root in Jesus Christ; and he said, "If anyone is in Christ, there is a new creation; everything old has passed away; see, everything has become new! All this is from God" (2 Corinthians 5:17-18). In Christ, all creation could be remade. As at the creation of the world all were formed to be in community with God, so in Christ is such community re-established. Adam and Eve walked in the garden of Eden with God. So too will God's people see God face to face in Christ.

Contrast how God sees us and how we see ourselves. God created us in God's own image. In God's eyes, we are the children of God and just a little less than angels. Yet, like Adam and Eve before us, we each want to be our own gods, to operate independently from God's vision for us.

Think about how people today are tempted to see themselves. For example, through the Internet, people connect with one another through online dating services or Facebook or other social networking sites in which fake pictures are shown, limitations overlooked, and falsehoods told freely. Online everybody can present themselves as more attractive, more accomplished, and more appealing than they are. Many times, people refuse to list their failures, their broken relationships, and their warts.

Yet God knows us as we are, counts every hair on our heads, and sees every failure in our lives. Sometimes, however, we forget these things and imagine that God expects us to be something other than we are before we receive God's love and forgiveness.

Ignoring God's grace, we suspect that God is searching for ideal Christian disciples. Think about it. How might God advertise for disciples with clean records of behavior? Certainly no lying, stealing, cheating, smoking, drinking, or cussing would be allowed. No personal failures such as job loss, failing grades, or broken relationships would be allowed either.

In addition, surely, God would accept only disciples already committed to daily prayer and Bible study; large, sacrificial gifts to the church; and extraordinary service to the poor. The more prospective disciples resemble someone like Mother Teresa the better. Furthermore, disciples should be multitalented. The people God would choose as disciples would already be great speakers, teachers, and administrators. At the same time, they would be able to sing in the choir, cook for church dinners, build houses for the homeless, and get along with young and old alike.

Wait a minute! If God's personal ad for Christian disciples were to include all those criteria, there is no way anyone we know could apply. If God wants people who have always done everything right and who are already fully mature, talented, and committed Christians, then we do not have a chance. Not one of us is perfect. We have all failed to love and serve God faithfully, not just once but over and over again. So if God is looking for perfection, then we certainly do not qualify.

God's chosen people of Israel were hardly the cream of the crop. Abraham was one hundred years old, and Sarah was ninety when God overcame their infertility and gave them a son named Isaac. Moses was a murderer hiding out in the wilderness of Midian when God spoke to him in a burning bush. Rahab was a Canaanite prostitute, but God chose her house as a hideout for the Israelites when they came to Jericho. David was an adulterer and a murderer, but God allowed him to remain king of Israel and to bear a son named Solomon.

Those are just a few of the people God chose to bless. Over and over again God called ordinary, imperfect people into a loving relationship with God. Time and again, God's people sinned and turned away from God; but God chose to love them. The wonderful and amazing truth is that God chooses to love us just as we are.

God sent Jesus into the world so that people might understand once and for all that God chooses to love all human beings. Paul makes it clear that God's love and reconciliation through Jesus Christ makes a new creation and a new people.

Paul wrote from his own experience. He was a religious leader dedicated to persecuting Christians when on the road to Damascus to arrest and persecute Christians, he heard Christ calling him. In a flash of light Paul was transformed (Acts 9:1-9), but that was just the beginning of God's work in Paul's life. Instead of persecuting Christians, Paul became one of Christianity's most effective missionaries ever, teaching, preaching, and founding churches throughout the Mediterranean world.

We cannot earn God's love and forgiveness any more than Paul could, and we do not have to earn God's love. God chooses to love us just as we are. That is the gospel of reconciliation that Paul proclaimed.

However, being reconciled to God as individuals is not the end of the story. When Paul and the Corinthians were baptized, they were commissioned by God to be ministers of God's love in their day-to-day lives, to bring about the same reconciliation in the lives of others that they themselves so graciously had received (2 Corinthians 5:18-19). Paul did not see in Corinth a city full of sinners but a people full of potential. Paul overlooked the corruption of Corinth and saw the possibilities of a vital and vibrant congregation.

The Spirit of God is working within us as well, empowering us to be the ministers God has commissioned us to be. We see one another not with our warts and shortcomings but in the image of God. We overlook one another's failures and see the good in one another. We do not see society as beyond help but through God's transforming love, capable of great good.

How could you be different if you acknowledged your reconciliation with God and shared that reconciliation with others? How could your reconciliation with God affect your family, your church, and your community?

THE EXTRAVAGANT FATHER
LUKE 15:1-3, 11b-32

Jesus' story of an extravagant father with two sons is one of the most beautiful stories ever told. In just a few hundred words, we hear about youthful disobedience, life in distress, fatherly love, sibling rivalry, and more. Jesus reminds all of us that God's love is not either/or but both/and, not just for wayward children but also unrepentant siblings, not just for sinners but also for saints.

During his journey to Jerusalem, Jesus had been healing and teaching; and thousands of people had now gathered around him. At the start of the story, the Pharisees, who were known to be properly religious, ordinary people, and even the sinful tax collectors were crowding around Jesus. Whom would Jesus welcome? Whom would he allow around the table? Many of us have heard this story so many times with a focus on the rebellious younger son or on the faithful older son that we forget that the story is addressed to each of us. Jesus invites everyone, including all of us, to the table.

In Jesus' day and time leaving home was not a natural rite of passage. Today, we expect young adults to leave the family nest and explore the world. In biblical culture, however, sons were expected to marry and bring their wives home. It was normal for multiple generations to live in one house.

Yet, in this story, the younger son destroyed the family into which he had been born. The younger son asked for his inheritance, one third of the family property, and promptly left the family estate and wasted away his money. Essentially, the younger son betrayed his father and family; and through his disrespectful actions he communicated this message to his father: "Drop dead."

For a while, the son had a great time: eating, spending, drinking, and living it up. However, his fun lasted only as long as his money; and it was not long before he was destitute and forced to take a job feeding pigs. Remember that this young man was Jewish. Jews considered pigs unclean and unfit for eating. By working on a pig farm, he had wandered as far as he possibly could from his father's house and values.

Confronted by misfortune and famine, the younger son came to his senses. Many of us know that experience. When we travel in the wrong direction and end up in a distant country, we feel guilt, shame, and a sense of homelessness. What we need is help. In his pain, the younger son remembered his father's love. He left behind the pigpen and returned home.

The homecoming scene is unexpected. A dignified Palestinian landowner, clothed in long, flowing robes, would never have run to meet anyone. However, this loving father had been searching the horizon for his son every day. He had not locked the doors or extinguished the candles in the windows but had been watching constantly for his son's return home. That is why the father set aside his pride and ran with wild

abandon to meet the son who had humiliated him.

The younger son probably had a speech of remorse all prepared, but the father did not wait to hear it. Instead, the father threw his arms around his son and hugged him tight. "Quick!" the father called to the servants. "Bring the best robe and put it on him. Put a ring on his finger and sandals on his feet. Bring the fattened calf and kill it. Let's have a feast and celebrate. For this son of mine was dead and is alive again; he was lost and is found."

The story is not over. There is the older son to consider. The father had plundered the possessions of the older son for the sake of the runaway boy. The feast with the calf started without inviting the stay-at-home child. He was livid with anger. The older son was so inflated by his sense of entitlement that he refused to eat with his brother, who in his mind had not earned a place at the table. The father loved the younger son, but he loved the older son every bit as much. The father wanted that son at the table, too.

There are many stories in our culture that are variations on the theme of going home. The story of finding one's way home is the story of Dorothy in *The Wizard of Oz* and of Ebenezer Scrooge in *A Christmas Carol* in prose. Jesus' story is a profound witness to the God who greets us and reconciles us when we come home. The word *prodigal* means "extravagant." While Jesus' parable does speak of the wasteful extravagance of the younger son, ultimately the parable is a story about the wonderful and extravagant love of the father and even more so the wonderful and extravagant love of God.

Lent is the season for coming to the feast. God welcomes all people to the feast. God invites us to sit at a table crowded with saints and sinners. No matter where we go, no matter what we do, no matter how we act, no matter how we look, no matter what sins we commit, no matter how good we are, there is room for us at God's table.

Where are you in the story? Are you the rebellious younger son who has wandered far from God or the stay-at-home son who expects a blessing? What does the story say about God's love for you?

Worship the Lord

Scriptures for Lent: The Fifth Sunday
Isaiah 43:16-21
Philippians 3:4b-14
John 12:1-8

In each of the Scriptures for this fifth Sunday of Lent, we are invited to marvel in God's grace and to worship the God who is even now at work in our midst.

Isaiah 43:16-21 tells about God's power to transform. The seventh-century prophet explained to the Israelites that they would soon be witnesses to a new exodus. Just as God had acted powerfully to rescue the people from slavery in Egypt, so too would God act powerfully to lead the people out of slavery in Babylon and back to the holy city of Jerusalem. Just as God had blessed the people in exile in Egypt, so too would God bless the people in exile in Babylon.

For Isaiah, God was worthy of Israel's praise in Babylon as well as for the mighty acts God performed in the days of Moses. As Isaiah assured the Israelites, God's power was not confined to the past. God was "about to do a new thing"; God would "make a way in the wilderness and rivers in the desert" and would lead the people home (Isaiah 43:19).

In Philippians 3:4b-14, Paul writes of his personal transformation from a fierce opponent of Christianity to a devoted follower of the Lamb of God. No longer did he value the righteousness he had obtained by following the Law. Of far greater value were his relationship with Jesus Christ and the righteousness he was receiving as a gift through faith in Christ.

Paul, too, knew that God was worthy of praise. He summoned the Philippians to overlook their trials and tribulations and to focus instead on God's transformation of each of them into a child of God. They could "worship in the Spirit of God and boast in Christ Jesus" (Philippians 3:3), not because they had followed the Law and had been circumcised but because Jesus had made them his own through his death and resurrection.

In John 12:1-8, Mary had not yet witnessed Jesus' self-giving death on the cross; but when Jesus raised her brother, Lazarus, from the dead, she experienced firsthand Jesus' love for her and her family.

In order to demonstrate her devotion to Jesus, Mary anointed his feet with perfume. Jesus had raised Lazarus from the dead; and in heart-felt response, Mary, the sister of Lazarus, washed Jesus' feet with expensive perfume and dried them with her hair. Mary offered much more to Jesus than the gift of perfume; she offered to Jesus her very self. To thank Jesus, Mary knelt before him and worshiped.

As we journey toward Easter, we reflect on these Scriptures and learn what it means to respond to God with worship. We discover the power of God in our lives so we, too, might respond with worship.

A NEW THING
ISAIAH 43:16-21

The Book of Isaiah is often divided by scholars into three parts: Chapters 1–39 reflect the years leading up to Israel's exile in Babylon and speak of God's judgment. Chapters 40–55 were written during the final years of exile and proclaim God's comfort. Chapters 56–66 mirror the early years following the people's return to Israel and witness to continued hope that God will yet redeem wayward Israel.

The 66 chapters of Isaiah cover several hundred years of Israel's history; and for that reason, most scholars conclude that more than one prophet penned the collection of oracles we now call the Book of Isaiah. Even so, the same basic message of God's work of salvation is woven throughout the pages of the book.

Isaiah 43:16-21 is included in the section that offers comfort to God's people forty or fifty years after Judah and Jerusalem had been destroyed by the Babylonians and many of the Israelites had been deported to Babylon. The people doubted they were God's chosen people. They even doubted if God had the power to save them from bondage and restore their beloved home.

Isaiah and other prophets had warned Israel that its destruction was imminent. Previous generations had forgotten the covenant God made with Moses. Judges, kings, priests, and the whole people of the covenant had violated God's laws. In 587 B.C., enemy armies had destroyed the Temple, dismantled the walls of Jerusalem, and seized the nation's leaders and carted them off to serve as slaves in a foreign land. The people understood this destruction and exile as the consequence of breaking God's covenant. Would God once again free God's people? Isaiah declared that God would rescue and redeem them.

Isaiah's words are based upon faith in God's steadfast love for Israel and in the fact that God had already acted to save the people a thousand years earlier. These verses from Isaiah 43 recall the first Exodus with the miraculous parting of the waters, which brought deliverance for the Israelites but total destruction for the Egyptian army.

God then provided water and manna to keep the people going through forty years of desert wanderings. It was God's triumph over

Egypt that gave confidence that God also would be victorious over the Babylonians.

This new exodus from Babylon, however, would be different than the first. Forget about the past: "Do not remember the former things, or consider the things of old." That is because God was "about to do a new thing; now it springs forth, do you not perceive it?" (verses 18-19). God would soon establish a new relationship between God and Israel. The prophet Jeremiah understood God's new thing as a new covenant (Jeremiah 31:31-34).

The psalm for today also expresses a sense of gratitude for God's past and future blessings. Psalm 126 was probably sung as the people of Israel walked up the mountainside to Solomon's Temple before the Babylonian exile and again after the second Temple was built. The psalm expresses joy in a time of deliverance (verses 1-3).

At times, we may also wonder about God's presence in our lives. When terrorists strike our nation, when a loved one dies, when a relationship ends, when the weak are overlooked, and when our prayers go unanswered, where is God? Isaiah's recurring image of water helps us remember our personal covenant with God. We are also spiritual heirs of the liberation from Egypt and Babylon. It is through water and the Holy Spirit that we became children of God. German Reformer Martin Luther said that when our sins and conscience oppress us, we strengthen ourselves and take comfort and say, "I am baptized."[1]

Andy was baptized as an infant in 1953. Sally was baptized as a child in elementary school in 1963. Over the years, our parents often reminded us that through water and the Spirit we were children of God. In our moments of despair and joy, this promise of God remained steadfast.

At the baptisms of our two daughters, we claimed the promise that God would be part of their lives always. We are grateful that today our adult daughters know the presence of God in their lives. Our older daughter, Ann, is currently serving with her husband, Nathan, in the Peace Corps in Togo, West Africa. She is learning to live simply in a small African village even as she has the opportunity to teach life skills to young girls and women.

Our younger daughter, Sarah, is studying theology and international development in Washington, DC. Her goal is to work with women in developing countries. We are eager to see how God will continue to claim them as baptized children and to help them to grow and change.

As we continue our journey through Lent and toward Easter, following Jesus in his final journey, may we remember the Exodus and Israel's return from exile in Babylon. Like the people of Israel, we too can find solace and joy in the Holy One who "makes a way in the sea: a path in the mighty waters." We can celebrate God's steadfast love for us and offer God our praise and worship.

When has God made "a way in the sea" for you? How did you

experience God's presence? How did you respond to God? How might you respond now?

PRESS ON TOWARD THE GOAL
PHILIPPIANS 3:4B-14

This Sunday, we turn to Paul's letter to the new Christians in Philippi. Paul loved those early followers who had begun to transfer their allegiance from Rome to the kingdom of God. In this Scripture, Paul reminded the Philippians to hold fast to their faith whatever obstacles they faced.

If you visit Philippi today, you will find extensive ruins of a Roman amphitheater, library, and forum, which were all destroyed by the frequent earthquakes that rock that region of the world. Just outside the center of the city, archaeologists have excavated a small, caved-in building they call the Prison of Paul. The room is about ten feet wide, fifteen feet deep, and ten feet high. Covered by mud for over a thousand years, the prison was only uncovered in the last fifty years.

Paul understood his imprisonment, not as a sign of defeat and failure but as an opportunity to recognize God's presence in his life and to proclaim the gospel. Paul told the Philippians, "Because of my chains, most of the brothers and sisters have become confident in the Lord and dare all the more to proclaim the gospel without fear" (Philippians 1:14).

In Philippians 3:4-14, Paul recounted his spiritual journey. He spoke of himself as "circumcised on the eighth day, a member of the people of Israel, of the tribe of Benjamin, a Hebrew born of Hebrews; as to the law, a Pharisee; as to zeal, a persecutor of the church; as to righteousness under the law, blameless" (3:5-6). Yet, on the road to Damascus, the living Christ spoke to him and set him on a new path. No longer would he travel to persecute the Christians, but he would travel by foot and by boat to tell the good news of Jesus Christ.

As a Pharisee, Paul had achieved many things. We might compare Paul to a precocious adolescent who believed that he could do all things. Yet as an adult Paul set aside his pride and his accomplishments and sought transformation by Jesus Christ. Paul's prayer for the Philippians was that they, too, would be transformed, not through their own efforts but by the power of God in Christ.

Former US president Jimmy Carter described his conversion in his book *Living Faith.* Carter called this experience "an intimate melding of my life with that of Jesus: I become a brother with him, and God is our mutual parent." As Carter explained, "Being born again is a new life, not of perfection but of striving, stretching, and searching—a life of intimacy with God through the Holy Spirit. There must first be an emptying, and then a refilling. . . . For me, it has been an evolutionary thing. Rather than a flash of light or a sudden vision of God speaking, it involved a series of steps that have brought me steadily closer to Christ."[2]

Like Paul, some people have a bright moment of transformation, while others find their lives being gradually transformed throughout their lives, like Carter. How would you describe your transformation?

No matter how God goes about transforming our lives, the truth is that God does. As our lives are being transformed, the presence of Christ becomes real for each of us.

Paul was willing to give up all of his credentials as a Pharisee in order that he might experience Christ's presence and receive the gift of righteousness through the death and resurrection of Jesus Christ. Here is how Eugene Peterson paraphrases Paul's explanation to the Philippians: "I gave up all that inferior stuff so I could know Christ personally, experience his resurrection power, be a partner in his suffering, and go all the way with him to death itself. If there was any way to get in on the resurrection from the dead, I wanted to do it"[3] (Philippians 3:10-11, *The Message*).

What Paul received through a relationship with Jesus Christ was worth so much more than anything he had ever received through his own efforts. When we recognize the power of God at work in our lives, we too can see the worth and value of giving ourselves to Christ. The rewards far exceed the losses.

What choices or decisions can you make during Lent that will keep you open to God's transforming power? How do you see God's transforming power in your life?

ANOINTING JESUS' FEET
JOHN 12:1-8

Jesus arrived in Bethany, about two miles east of Jerusalem, just beyond the ridge of the Mount of Olives. The house he visited was a short distance over the hill from Jerusalem and beyond the city gate, through which he would soon enter in a procession of waving palms and shouts of praise. However, before beginning that fateful ride into Jerusalem, Jesus stopped for dinner at the home of his good friends Mary and Martha and their brother, Lazarus. This is the same Lazarus whom Jesus had raised from the dead just days before. Perhaps Lazarus hosted this dinner in order to thank Jesus for the unbelievable gift of life.

Can you imagine the sense of awe and joy in that room? As Lazarus welcomed the guests and Martha served the meal, Mary fell at the feet of Jesus to express her love for him by kneeling before him and washing his feet. In what would be perceived as an outrageous social action, Mary knelt before Jesus and poured expensive perfume on his feet. She then wiped them clean with her hair, and the house was filled with the wonderful fragrance of that perfume (John 12:3).

Mary's gift did not come cheaply. She anointed his feet with "a pound of costly perfume made of pure nard" (verse 3). As Judas was quick to point out, that perfume was worth three hundred denarii, which at the time was equivalent to a year's salary for an average worker. Anointing Jesus' feet with sweet-smelling perfume was an act of pure extravagance. What was more, by choosing to anoint Jesus' feet, Mary was setting herself up to be criticized, not only by Judas but by the other disciples as well. In first-century Palestine, servants or slaves were the ones who washed the feet of dinner guests.

However, Mary did not care about appearances. She did not care what other people thought—nobody other than Jesus, that is. Mary wanted Jesus to know how much she appreciated his care for her and her family, so she anointed Jesus' feet with perfume and wiped them dry with her hair; and Jesus gladly accepted Mary's extravagant gift of gratitude and love.

Anointing Jesus' feet with expensive perfume signified the depth of Mary's love for her friend Jesus, but what makes Mary's gift even more significant is that this precious ointment was often used at the burial of the dead. Perhaps the perfume had been purchased for the burial of Lazarus. Jesus remarked, "She bought it so that she might keep it for the day of my burial" (verse 7). Her action foreshadows the coming death of Jesus.

According to this Scripture, the disciple Judas had little understanding of Jesus' ministry. Judas criticized Mary, arguing that the perfume should have been sold to raise money for the poor. However, Judas was not worried about the needs of others; he was focused on himself and his own agenda (verse 6). It is not clear what the other disciples thought of Mary's extravagant gift of perfume,

but it is doubtful that they understood any better than Judas did how Jesus would soon pour out his life for them on the cross.

Mary's act of worship set the stage for Jesus' act of foot washing on the following Thursday night. As Mary got down on her knees before Jesus, so Jesus got down on his knees before his friends. As Mary washed Jesus' feet with ointment, so Jesus washed the feet of his disciples with water. As Mary dried Jesus' feet with her hair, so Jesus dried the disciples' feet with his garment. As Mary took the position of a servant to anoint Jesus' feet, so Jesus took the role of a servant to wash the feet of his disciples (13:1-20).

One of the great traditions of Holy Week occurs on Thursday. The service often held on this day is the Maundy Thursday service. Maundy Thursday signifies Jesus' new commandment (Latin, *mandatum novum*) in John 13:34 that the disciples love one another. Because Jesus washed the feet of his first disciples to express his love for them, many Christians all over the world express their love for Jesus and one another on Maundy Thursday by washing one another's feet.

Every year we have foot-washing services in our congregations. Typically, we start with the children, inviting them to come down and take off their shoes. We wash their feet and then let them wash our feet. We then invite their parents and others to join us. Typically, most people's first reactions include nervous laughter. Who wants to see, let alone wash, somebody else's feet? Yet the very act of

Baptism - Symbol of cleansing

"sense of entitlement"
of deserving of
His love & inheritance
offered

holding someone's feet, bathing them in warm water, and then drying them with a towel brings forth a new appreciation and love for one another. Opening ourselves to serve one another in humility opens us to an attitude of worship and respect for the One who serves all of us.

How do we worship the Savior of the world? As we draw near to Holy Week, do we respond to Jesus as Mary did, as Judas did, or as the disciples did? Do we stand with Judas and complain about the expense? Do we simply continue living our lives as if nothing has happened, or do we kneel beside Mary and offer our complete discipleship? Do we worship him, challenge him, or ignore him? Do we wash the feet of our fellow Christians?

Through Jesus, God offers life and a complex web of nurturing relationship with God and with one another. Jesus stands beside us in our darkest hours. Jesus gave us the ultimate gift: his body and blood. As we recognize these amazing gifts, our hearts, like Mary's, can respond with love, gratitude, and worship.

In what ways can you identify with Mary's story? When was your heart overflowing with gratitude? How did you thank Jesus? What gift can you offer in Jesus' name?

[1] From *The Large Catechism,* by Martin Luther (*iclnet.org/pub/resources/text/ wittenberg/luther/catechism/web/cat-13.html*).
[2] From *Living Faith,* by Jimmy Carter (Times Books, 1996); pages 20-22.
[3] Scripture quotations from *THE MESSAGE.* Copyright © by Eugene H. Peterson 1993, 1994, 1995, 1996, 2000, 2001, 2002. Used by permission of NavPress Publishing Group.

Celebrate and Mourn

Scriptures for Lent:
The Sixth Sunday
Isaiah 50:4-9a
Philippians 2:5-11
Luke 22:14–23:56

Today's Scriptures embody the sharp contrasts of Holy Week. In Luke 19:29-40, we journey with Jesus in a joyous demonstration of love as he enters Jerusalem. As he arrived on the back of a donkey, the people shouted, "Blessed is the King who comes in the name of the Lord!" However, the story does not end with the celebration. In Luke 22:14–23:56, we also journey with Jesus through the Last Supper, prayer on the Mount of Olives, betrayal and arrest, denial, mocking and beating, trials, imprisonment, crucifixion, death, and burial. What begins with celebration leads to mourning.

Surrounding this Passion-tide text are powerful Scriptures that reinforce the themes of the day. In Isaiah 50:4-9, we read about the suffering servant, who modeled for the Israelites in exile a lifestyle of trusting obedience to God. Years later, the Chosen One of God would embody best the attributes of a servant. Jesus would lead God's people, not as the head of a military and political movement but as a suffering and trusting servant.

Philippians 2:5-11 includes a highly poetic section commonly thought of as a hymn[1] in which Paul invited the early Christians to take on the example of Christ's suffering so that these early followers might claim his glory. During Lent, we are reminded that for us, too, the way to the crown of glory is always the way of the cross.

In the last years of his life, Andy's father began to write poetry. While attending a Maundy Thursday service, he wrote a poem called "The Day of Death" on the back of a church bulletin:

We are not capable of Holy Week—
Its range too broad, its heights transcend us,
  its depths beyond our depth,
    its intensity too strong, its claims too great.
We move through the culminating days.
A triumphal entry, psalms and psalmists,
  the temple widows with too little money,
    money changers with too much.
A disciple meal, a Passover remembrance
  of God's saving act, anticipation
    of God's saving act.
The loneliness of being misunderstood
  forsaken in small things,
    forsaken in large things.

Capture, turmoil, trial, condemnation.
Crucifixion.
Burial.
He is more than we can comprehend.

Thomas A. Langford, Jr.
March 27, 1997
(Unpublished)

Through prayer and reflection on these Scriptures, may our journeys with Christ become more intense, more real, and more life-changing. The Lord has arrived in Jerusalem in glory and is journeying on to death on the cross.

CONFIDENCE IN GOD
ISAIAH 50:4-9a

This year during Lent, we read the third of four servant songs from Isaiah (Isaiah 42:1-4; 49:1-6; 50:4-9; and 52:13–53:12). Isaiah 50:4-9a is a poignant cry in which the servant proclaims ongoing trust in God even in the face of severe opposition. Christians view the suffering of Jesus through the lens of this servant song.

The context for all four of these songs is the Babylonian exile during the sixth century before Christ. The Temple in Jerusalem had been destroyed and with it the people's confidence that the worship of the Lord of the covenant was still possible. Many Israelites had been deported to Babylon, and a secure and blessed life in the Promised Land had become a distant memory. The people of God questioned God's love for them. Had God rejected them? Was it possible to "sing the LORD's song in a foreign land"? (Psalm 137:4).

The prophet Isaiah assured the Israelites that God had not forgot-ten them. Indeed, their suffering in exile would be redemptive, if only they trusted in God's power to turn around their hopeless circumstances.

The servant songs in Isaiah point to the example of the suffering servant. His own dispirited people had abused the servant; but like a wounded hero, the servant had not stopped trusting in God, who sustained and ultimately would vindicate the servant.

The identity of the suffering servant is unknown. Was he a faithful individual, maybe a king or a prophet; or did he represent the ideal Israel? No one can say for sure; but in any case, the servant was called by God to embody for others the covenant commandments, originally revealed to Israel through Moses and later interpreted by the prophets.

In Isaiah 50:4-9, the suffering servant reflects on the painful lesson he was taught by the master, God. As a student, the servant "was not rebellious" and "did not turn backward" when "morning by morning he [God] wakens— wakens my ear to listen as those who are taught" (verses 4-5). The objective of the master's lesson was specific: to teach the student "how to sustain the weary with a word" (verse 4). The student listened and learned the master's lesson well.

God's purpose is for the student to become a servant and ultimately a teacher of redemptive suffering himself. Mere talk about trusting God would not be sufficient. No, the servant must model trust for Israel and the nations. The only way to do that was to remain faithful to God even in the midst of pain, disgrace, and rejection. That is why the servant "gave [his] back to those who struck [him], and [his] cheeks to those who pulled out the beard."

In order to draw those who were weary into a trusting relationship with God, the servant must not "hide [his] face from insult and spitting" (verse 6). Yet the suffering of the servant had meaning. The student trusted the teacher to vindicate and make the suffering redemptive. The master would not let the student suffer in vain. Through the servant's example, others would also experience a renewed trust in the Lord God.

Every prophet in the Old Testament must be read with two sets of eyes. First, what was the prophet saying about the immediate situation of the people of Israel? Second, how do we as Christians read the prophets' words? In the case of the servant songs in Isaiah, we read and receive insights about Jesus. We do not have to choose between them but choose instead to read the prophet Isaiah through both of these lenses.

Using the first set of lenses, we learn that Isaiah gave hope to the Israelites in exile in Babylon. The prophet or the Jewish people as a whole were the suffering servants. Isaiah's hope was justified when Cyrus rose to power in Babylon and allowed the people to return to Israel under the leadership of Ezra and Nehemiah.

This servant song can also give us guidance during Lent as we reflect on our journey with Jesus to the cross. On the first Sunday in Lent, we read in Luke 4 of Jesus' struggle with the devil in the wilderness. Confronted by real temptation, Jesus, the true servant, trusted only in God. On the second Sunday in Lent, Jesus was threatened by "that fox" Herod; but in the face of danger, Jesus declared that God alone was in control of his destiny. Throughout our Lenten journey, we have been reminded that Jesus is the true servant who takes on pain and rejection in order to draw people, including tax collectors and sinners, into a redemptive relationship with God.

Isaiah 50:4-9 clearly prepares us for Jesus' experience in the garden of Gethsemane, his trials before the religious and political authorities, and his crucifixion at Golgotha. Just as Isaiah's servant taught others by his steady focus on God in the midst of suffering, so too did Jesus teach others through his faithful stance in that lonely garden at the foot of the Mount of Olives, before those religious and political leaders who opposed him, and along the stone path to his death on the cross. Through his suffering, God prepared Jesus for his Passion and Jesus taught his disciples to be ready also.

Throughout our lives, we have known persons who understood what it means to be a suffering servant. They trusted in God when it would have made sense to others for them to question God's faithfulness. We remember two parents who cared without complaining for their child who was born with a birth defect and needed constant attention. Their original dream for their child may be lost, but they have discovered joy in the limited successes of their child. We also have friends who gave up lucrative, professional jobs to follow God and go into full-time ministry.

Then there are the families we know who choose to spend their summer vacations, not at the beach or on a cruise but in depressed locations around the country, working with children in need. We can name family members and friends who have faced illnesses and death with remarkable grace and good cheer. Because of their trust in God's never-dying love, we have renewed hope.

When has someone else's trust in God, even in the midst of undeserved suffering, deepened your faith in God? When you are weary, broken, and hurt, how do you experience God? How is God present for you in the midst of such suffering?

THE MIND OF CHRIST
PHILIPPIANS 2:5-11

Paul was in prison when he wrote the letter to the Christians in Philippi, which was a leading city on the northeastern coast of Greece. Paul had founded the church in Philippi, and over the years he had developed a close relationship with the congregation.

The Philippians, like Paul, faced constant opposition and persecution by non-Christian officials. Paul wrote these Christian friends to encourage them to stand firm in their faith. Paul assured the con-gregation that even in prison his joy in the Lord remained strong. God had raised Jesus from the dead. Because of God's victory over death, they too should face the future with the mind of Christ.

Philippians 2:5-11, commonly called a hymn, summarized the person and work of Jesus the Christ. At baptism and upon entry into the Christian faith, new believers confessed that Jesus was their savior; but what kind of savior was Jesus? The hymn declares that before the Incarnation, Jesus was of equal status with God; but Jesus humbled himself and became human. Although he was equal to God, Jesus willingly suffered and died.

That is not, of course, where this Christian hymn ends the story of Jesus. Jesus died, but now God has raised Jesus from the dead. God has given Jesus "the name that is above every name, so that at the name of Jesus every knee should bend, in heaven and on earth and under the earth, and every tongue should confess that Jesus Christ is Lord, to the glory of God the Father" (verses 9-11).

The language in the beginning words of the hymn is similar to the language of the first chapter of The Gospel According to John: "In the beginning was the Word, and the Word was with God, and the Word was God" (John 1:1).

Unlike the birth narratives in Matthew and Luke, John's Gospel expresses the belief of early Christians that Jesus was there at the creation of the world. Jesus, the Word, "was in the beginning with God"; and "all things came into being through him, and without him not one thing came into being" (John 1:3). Jesus was there when God created order out of chaos and brought forth life on the earth. Then in the fullness of time "the Word became flesh and lived among us, and we have seen his glory, the glory as of a father's only son, full of grace and truth" (John 1:14).

The Word became incarnate in a Child born in a manger. The humility of Jesus' birth was followed by the obedience of his death. The Greek word used for Jesus' act of humiliation and self-giving is *kenosis*.

The key word in the hymn is the word *therefore*. From the construction of the hymn, we may think that the Passion of the Christ simply preceded his glorification. He suffered and died, and then he gained his reward. The Greek conjunction for *therefore*, however, is not temporal but causative. Christ's suffering unto death did not simply come before his glory but instead was the very reason that he gained his full glory. Jesus Christ's exaltation as Lord of the universe came precisely because he became human and suffered death on the cross.

Simply said, without the cross, there is no glory. Without humiliation and death, there is no exaltation and life.

Paul reminded the Christians of Philippi that Jesus did not simply take on the outward form of a slave. No, when Jesus healed the hungry, fed the sick, and ate with sinners, when Jesus served others to the point of death on the cross, he revealed his true nature. While Jesus never sought recognition for his loving servitude, God highly exalted him; and one day all people, including the Philippian Christians, will confess Jesus Christ as Lord.

Paul and the Philippians needed to sing this hymn over and over again. In Philippians 1, we see that the threat of persecution hovered over the community. Such suffering was not something to be merely tolerated and endured. Paul understood suffering as the very passageway into the kingdom of God.

The early Christians had hope because Jesus Christ had prepared the way. Paul's shipwrecks, stoning, beatings, and imprisonments were experiences in which he discovered the glories of following Jesus. The suffering of the Philippians could also be their passage into life. Paul told them to stand firm because God had granted them "the privilege not only of believing in Christ, but of suffering for him as well" (verses 28-29).

Throughout our ministries, we have encountered persons who have discovered the truth of Paul's message. In the midst of suffering and pain, broken relationships, and unfulfilled dreams, these women and men have experienced joy and triumph, not despair and defeat. A cancer survivor becomes a healer. A person abused as a child becomes a teacher. Persons who know what it is to go without become sacrificial givers.

Paul teaches us that God's redeeming power of life is with us even through times of suffering. Following Jesus' example of humility opens our minds and hearts to the power and glory of God revealed in him.

How might you express the mind of Christ in your daily life? What would change? What would remain the same? How might you look to the interests of others as Jesus did?

THE PASSION OF CHRIST
LUKE 22:14–23:56

Several years ago, worship began on Passion/Palm Sunday at First United Methodist Church in China Grove, North Carolina, much as it does each year in other churches. The mood in the church was joyful. The biblical story of Jesus' triumphal entry into Jerusalem was read aloud; and then the children's and adult choirs processed down the center aisle of the sanctuary, waving palm branches and singing, "All Glory, Laud, and Honor." Accompanied by brass and organ, the choirs and congregation sang the processional hymn with heartfelt enthusiasm.

The mood of the worship service became more somber, however, when the story of Jesus' arrest and crucifixion was presented as a dramatic reading. Several individuals, dressed simply in black, sat on stools in the chancel area and read the account of Jesus' Passion from the Gospel According to Luke. One person read the narration, while others read the parts of Jesus, Peter, Judas, the servant girl, Pilate, Herod, the crowd, and the centurion.

The reading of Jesus' Passion took all of us worshipers that day by surprise. We had thought we were faithful disciples, following Jesus with shouts of adoration,

"Hosanna to the Son of David!" As the story unfolded, however, we realized anew that we were the people who rejected Jesus and nailed him to the cross. When we were baptized and joined the church, we confessed Jesus Christ as our Savior and promised to serve him as our Lord. However, through our thoughts and actions, we worshipers knew that we had shouted over and over again with the crowd, "Crucify him! Crucify him!"

So often, unfortunately, congregations jump from the glorious music and pageantry of Palm Sunday to the magnificent joy of Easter Sunday. They miss the impact of Jesus' arrest and crucifixion altogether. In the early years of the church, however, all Christians observed a Holy Week, attended worship daily, and remembered what happened between the two great festivals of Palm Sunday and Easter Sunday: the suffering and death of Jesus. One third of each of the Gospel accounts focuses on these few holy days.

This year's Scripture from Luke —114 verses in Chapters 22 and 23 —present the climax of the story of Jesus. We invite you simply to read the Scripture aloud, slowly and meditatively, while you savor and reflect upon each word. Here is the outline of the story:

Luke 22:14-23—The Last Supper. On Thursday evening, Jesus and his friends gathered for a Passover meal. During the meal, Jesus indicated that one of them would soon betray him. Luke names this final supper as a Passover meal, clearly linking Jesus to the Exodus and the freedom festival. Paul also used this Scripture as the foundation of his explanation of the Lord's Supper in 1 Corinthians 10.

At the Passover meal, Jesus shared a cup of wine and broken bread with his friends in order to remind them of the offering of his life on their behalf. The journey of Jesus' life was almost over. Jesus' sharing of bread and wine with his disciples would be remembered on Holy Thursday when Christians around the world celebrate Holy Communion.

Luke 22:24-38—True discipleship. As the disciples quarreled about their place in the new Kingdom, Jesus reminded them that the way of service and self-denial is the way of Christ, the message also proclaimed by Isaiah and Paul. Peter promised Jesus that he would follow him to prison and death, but Jesus replied that Peter would deny him three times before the cock crowed. Jesus warned all of the disciples that true discipleship would be met with violent resistance.

Luke 22:39-53—The Mount of Olives. On that Thursday night, we feel the agony of our Lord as we read Jesus' prayer: "Father, if you are willing, remove this cup from me; yet, not my will but yours be done" (verse 42). There in the place that Matthew and Mark call Gethsemane, Jesus indicated that he could have escaped his suffering and death; yet Jesus did not use his relationship with God as a way to avoid suffering. Instead, Jesus fully accepted God's plan for him and trusted that through death he would bring life to God's people.

After praying, Jesus found all of the disciples sleeping. Even as he was waking them, Judas arrived with a crowd from the Temple; and Judas betrayed Jesus with the kiss remembered throughout history.

Luke 22:54-62—Peter's denial. Peter's weakness was not meekness but cowardice. Unlike Jesus, Peter refused to take on the mantle of humility or follow in the footsteps of his master. Initially, of course, Peter boldly affirmed his devotion to Jesus. Unfortunately, Peter deserted Jesus in his hours of greatest need. Peter claimed to be a faithful disciple; but at the time of Jesus' arrest, Peter's discipleship faltered.

Luke 22:63-71—Jesus' trial. In the middle of the night, Jesus was mocked by the Temple police and stood trial before the Sanhedrin, the religious leaders in Jerusalem. Jesus was accused, jailed, tortured, challenged, and found guilty by religious leaders who saw him as a threat to their authority. At stake was his identity as Messiah.

Luke 23:1-25—Jesus with Pilate and Herod. Jesus was confronted by the political power of Rome. He faced the Roman governor and also the puppet ruler of the Jews—Herod. The fox and the hen were now face to face. Who would prove to be the king of the world? While neither Herod nor Pilate believed the charges against Jesus, they yielded to the demands of the populace.

Luke 23:26-43—The way of the cross. In route to his execution, Jesus carried his own instrument of torture and execution, the cross. As he carried his cross, Jesus was assisted by Simon of Cyrene. The distance from the Roman palace to the hillside outside the city may have been only a few hundred yards. Yet, having been beaten and whipped, each step for Jesus would have been torture.

When Jesus arrived at Calvary, two criminals argued over who Jesus was. The heartfelt words of one of them, "Jesus, remember me" (verse 42), are remembered as a simple but profound prayer for mercy.

Luke 23:44-56—The death and burial. At three o'clock in the afternoon, Jesus died with an anguished cry of trust in God: "Father, into your hands I commend my spirit" (verse 46). In the most poignant scene of Mel Gibson's movie *The Passion of the Christ*, we watch a single tear fall from heaven at the moment of Jesus' death. God wept at the death of God's Son. The body was placed in a tomb. Could that be the end of the story of Jesus?

We have journeyed from celebration to mourning. As we enter Holy Week, we put off until Easter Sunday our enjoyment of beautiful lilies, delicious chocolate bunnies, and new spring clothes. We focus instead on the offering of Jesus the Christ. The bright flowers and glorious music can wait. Now is the time we reflect on the pain and suffering of the cross and the depth of God's love for the world.

In what way does the story of the suffering and death of Jesus help you grasp the depth of God's love? Which part of the narrative speaks most deeply to your journey through Lent? Why?

---

[1] From *The New Interpreter's Study Bible*; pages 2102-2103.

Celebrate the Resurrection

Scriptures for Easter:
Acts 10:34-43
1 Corinthians 15:19-26
Luke 24:1-12

The journey is complete. The Exile has ended. The wilderness has been left behind. We have come out of the dark woods into a marvelous light. The rock has been removed. The grave is empty. The new Kingdom shines before us. Christ is risen!

On this Easter Sunday, we celebrate that Jesus' life of sacrificial love ended not in death but in triumph. Think back on the events of the last few days in our churches. On Maundy Thursday we washed feet, celebrated Holy Communion, and stripped the sanctuary of its paraments and candles. On Good Friday, we walked with Jesus to Calvary where he died on the cross. The stone was rolled in front of the tomb. On Holy Saturday, the sanctuary and the world were dark. However, the powers of evil and death were not victorious. God raised Jesus from the dead.

Today is packed full of sleepy yet expectant eyes at sunrise. There will be bright flowers, new clothes, triumphal organ music, glorious singing, and joyful trumpets and trombones.

Most of us will see large crowds of people at worship on Easter Sunday. Faithful, longtime members of the church sometimes make comments about the greater number of people who come to worship only on Easter Sunday. "It is great to have a packed sanctuary," they say. "But shouldn't these people come to church every Sunday? Don't they know that being a Christian is not a once-a-year thing?"

Of course, it would be wonderful if our worship services were crowded with people every Sunday of the year; but in the final analysis, Easter Sunday is not about our faithfulness in coming to church. Easter Sunday focuses instead on the proclamation of the gospel of Jesus Christ, which is welcoming good news for us all.

On Easter Sunday, we keep our focus on the power of almighty God. Jesus died and then rose from the dead for the faithful and for the faithless. Jesus died and rose again for people who fought him every step of the way. Jesus died and lives for people who denied, betrayed, and deserted him. Jesus died for us but not because of our love for Jesus, but because of Jesus' love for us.

In Acts 10:34-43, Peter's speech to Cornelius's household reminds us that "God shows no partiality" (Acts 10:34). The good news of Christ's resurrection is for everyone. Paul reminds us that through the resurrection of Jesus Christ, "all will be made alive in Christ" (1 Corinthians 15:22). In Luke 24:1-12, when the women discover an empty tomb, we hear the angels tell them, "He is not here, but has risen" (Luke 24:5).

GOD SHOWS NO PARTIALITY
ACTS 10:34-43

Acts tells the story of the emerging church from the ascension of Christ through Paul's journey to Rome. The stories tell of Stephen's martyrdom, the first great church council, and Paul's travels throughout the Roman Empire. Throughout the church's history, during the season of Easter, Christians have replaced the readings from the Old Testament with readings from Acts. Why? The church itself, the living body of Christ, is the ongoing sign of Jesus' resurrection from the dead.

Today's verses from Acts 10 conclude the chapter-long story of the decision to spread Christianity to every person around the world. Jesus' disciple Peter was a member of the Jewish-Christian community in Jerusalem. All of Jesus' disciples had been Jews, and it is under-standable that many followers at first assumed that Christian converts must first become Jews.

Yet God had other plans. At the beginning of the chapter, Peter had a vision in which clean and unclean animals were all gathered together in a net from heaven. The vision from God challenged not only Jewish dietary laws but also Peter's understanding of who could be welcomed by the people of the Way.

No sooner had Peter had this vision than a Roman soldier named Cornelius, who clearly belonged to an evil empire, came to Peter seeking assistance. Would Peter help him or turn him away? Could a Roman soldier, who was also a Gentile, receive blessings from Christ?

It is at this point in Acts 10 that Peter explained the universality of God's love. He told the story of Jesus, beginning with Jesus' baptism by John in the river Jordan. Peter described how Jesus shared the good news in Judea and Jerusalem. Although the religious and political leaders hanged Jesus on a cross, Jesus rose from the dead.

Peter told them about being among the witnesses who ate and drank with the risen Christ and that Jesus had commanded them to spread this message of forgiveness and new life. Who needs to hear the story of the Resurrection? Everyone! Peter understood that the Resurrection was not a quiet secret for a chosen few. The story of life beyond death must be proclaimed to Jews and Gentiles everywhere.

In one of our congregations, a new member had a dilemma. She had only recently experienced the presence of the risen Christ in her life. In response to God's love for her through Jesus Christ, this woman was baptized and joined the church. She loved coming to worship, participating in Bible studies, and sharing in the fellowship of Christian community.

Then a new neighbor moved into her neighborhood. The new neighbor was loud and demanding and, clearly, an outsider in the closely-knit neighborhood. When the new neighbor asked which church the member attended, she hesitated. Did she want this stranger to come to her beloved church? Was she willing to share with an outsider what mattered most to her? Yes. The church member had a Peter moment. She remembered the occasion when a neighbor invited her to church. Thanks to that person's hospitality, she had experienced God's love. How could she not share that love with others? The church member invited her new neighbor to go with her to church that next Sunday.

It is interesting to consider how far Peter came in his understanding of God's love at work through Jesus Christ. After Jesus' arrest in the garden of Gethsemane, Peter was afraid for his own life. Even as Jesus was being interrogated and beaten by the religious leaders, Peter denied three times that he even knew Jesus.

Early Sunday morning, however, following Jesus' crucifixion on Friday, Peter saw the empty tomb. Later that day, the risen Christ came and said to him and to the other disciples, "Peace be with you" (Luke 24:36). From that Sunday on, Peter became a changed man. He was fearless in his commitment to preaching the good news of Jesus' resurrection from the dead. Tradition has it that Peter followed Jesus so completely that he himself would later be crucified upside down in Jerusalem.

In today's Scripture, Peter eagerly shares the story of Jesus, first with Cornelius and then with all of Cornelius's household and guests. The good news of the Resurrection was too good for Peter to keep to himself.

What about us? We have heard the story of the Resurrection over and over again, year after year. Are we so excited about the resurrection of Jesus Christ that we are willing to invite friends, neighbors, and family members to worship during the season of Easter? Are we ready to share the message of God's saving love through Jesus Christ with the world? Are we ready to welcome everyone into the kingdom of God?

As Christians, we profess belief in the resurrection of Jesus Christ and believe that through Christ we will also experience resurrection. God offers life to all of us. So who among our friends and acquaintances longs to experience the joy of Easter? Can we be fearless enough to tell them about God's undying love? The experience of Easter Sunday is not for longtime members only. God calls us, as he called Peter, to tell others the story of Jesus.

How do you respond to Peter's understanding that God shows no partiality? What does the Scripture say to you about sharing the good news of life and hope? How might your words and actions offer this good news to others in your life?

ALIVE IN CHRIST
1 CORINTHIANS 15:19-26

Paul, even though he never met Jesus during his earthly ministry, understood the essential meaning of Jesus Christ. Instead of telling stories about Jesus' ministry and teachings, Paul emphasized the big picture and declared how Jesus' resurrection from the dead has changed all reality. While Paul could not describe how Jesus was raised from the dead, he did not doubt that Jesus was raised from the dead. He understood the risen Christ as the first fruits of God's new creation in which everyone may participate (1 Corinthians 15:20-23).

In 1 Corinthians 15, Paul addressed the persons in Corinth who doubted the resurrection of the dead. For Paul, the Resurrection was the foundation of the Christian faith. He knew that the power of the risen Christ turns lives around. Even more so, Paul saw Jesus Christ's death and resurrection transforming the whole universe. God's relationship with humanity and all of creation was being restored through Jesus Christ. Paul had grasped the true significance of Jesus' resurrection, and it was his goal to convince others of the significance of God's transforming work in Jesus Christ.

The Greeks described the power of death in an ancient story of the singer and golden lyre player Orpheus, who tried to overcome death. The story would have been familiar to those who lived in Corinth. Orpheus sang with a voice almost as beautiful as that of the gods. According to the story, Orpheus and Eurydice loved one another; but one day, Eurydice stepped on a poisonous snake and died. She descended into the underworld.

Orpheus refused to accept Eurydice's death and determined that he would use his best talents to retrieve his beloved from the dead. Orpheus found the entrance to the underworld. As he began his journey down into the earth, Orpheus sang and played his lyre. Because Hades was so taken with Orpheus's music, he gave Orpheus permission to lead Eurydice up to the earth's surface and back to life. There was one ground rule, however, which Orpheus had to follow. Eurydice would live again but only if Orpheus restrained himself from looking back on Eurydice during their journey to the surface of the earth.

Unfortunately, Orpheus failed to follow Hades's command. Just before the lovers reached the surface of the earth, Orpheus turned to catch a glance at Eurydice. Hades was merciless. Because Orpheus broke Hades's ground rule, Eurydice was forced back to the underworld, where she would remain forever.[1]

The story of Orpheus and Eurydice is a sad one; and the message was clear to the Greeks: Humans, even talented humans, have no hope of overcoming death. Paul told a different story.

Paul believed that Jesus of Nazareth was the very Son of God. Jesus was not just a special child or a miracle worker or a wise teacher or a moral guide or a social revolutionary. Jesus the Messiah was the very presence of God on earth. Even more so, Jesus, who had been crucified, who had died, and who had been buried, had been raised by God from the dead.

Because of Jesus Christ's death and resurrection, the most important gift God in Christ was offering to all people—to Paul, the Jews, and the Greeks in the first century, and to us and everybody else in the twenty-first century—was the gift of life beyond death. This theme is central to today's Scripture reading.

How did Paul know this truth of life beyond death? Paul listened to Peter, the other apostles, and hundreds of other people as they described their experiences with the resurrected Jesus. The witness of other Christians influenced Paul's understanding of Jesus.

In the final analysis, however, Paul knew that Jesus Christ was resurrected because he himself had personally spoken with Jesus on the road to Damascus (Acts 9). In the flash of a bright light, the Savior Jesus Christ spoke to Paul by name and called him to proclaim the good news. Paul based all of his preaching and teaching on this core truth of Jesus' resurrection.

Indeed, Paul staked his very life on his belief that Jesus had been raised from the dead; and because Christ lives, he and all other people live, too. Paul's message of the resurrection led Jews and Gentiles into their transforming relationships with the risen Lord.

Even though Jesus had been crucified, God raised him from the dead. For that reason, Paul and the Corinthian Christians could face their deaths without fear. Paul proclaimed, "From now on, therefore, we regard no one from a human point of view. . . . If anyone is in Christ, there is a new creation: everything old has passed away; see, everything has become new" (2 Corinthians 5:16-17). Furthermore, Paul and the Corinthian Christians would through Christ conquer death, too. Paul proclaimed that everyone who follows Jesus, including all of us who celebrate the Resurrection this Easter Sunday, will triumph over death.

As Paul explained it, redemption by God comes by grace through faith and is fail-proof and without precondition. Our life in Christ does not come from anything we have accomplished. Our salvation is a free gift from God, which can never be snatched away from us. Good Friday happened, but that is not the end of the story. Easter and resurrection stand triumphant for us and for all creation this day.

How does Paul's understanding of the resurrection of the dead offer insights to you about life after death? What does it mean to you to be "made alive in Christ"?

CHRIST IS RISEN
LUKE 24:1-12

On Good Friday, our sanctuaries were stripped of banners, flowers, and decorations as we focused on the cross. Darkness and death loomed heavy upon us, as we reflected on the Crucifixion. On Sunday morning, however, we welcome the rising of the sun and the resurrection of our Lord and Savior Jesus Christ. In the first centuries of the church, Christians gathered early on Easter morning and sang together an ancient hymn known as the "Exsultet."[2] The words, which you may wish to read with passion, express the Easter joy of Christians through the ages.

Some Christian congregations celebrate pre-dawn Easter services so worshipers might experience the transition from darkness and death to light and life. Andy and our daughter Ann once attended a Greek Orthodox Easter vigil in Nashville. The vigil lasted from midnight until 3:00 A.M. In a darkened sanctuary, we read Scripture, sang hymns, chanted the Exsultet, and lighted candles to greet the resurrected Christ.

In Sally's hometown, the community sunrise service on Easter Sunday was always held at the city cemetery. At dawn on Easter Sunday, with tombstones all around them, people came to worship. Many churches continue to hold their Easter sunrise services in cemeteries. Of course, the focus of these Easter sunrise services is life, not death. With tombstones or grave markers all around them,

Christians declare that death has no power over them. Jesus Christ has been raised from the dead; and because Christ lives, we live also.

Mary Magdalene, Joanna, Mary the mother of James, and the other women with them discovered an empty tomb on that first Easter morning. When the women came to Jesus' tomb at sunrise, death, not life, was heavy on their minds. On Friday, they had seen Jesus suffering and dying on the cross. They were there when Joseph of Arimathea took the bruised and lifeless body of Jesus, wrapped it in a linen cloth, and laid it in a rock-hewn tomb. They had watched as a huge stone was rolled across the tomb's opening.

When the women came to Jesus' tomb again on Sunday, death was all they could think of or imagine. They wept and mourned, and the world was for them one huge cemetery; but there at the tomb of Jesus the unthinkable happened: God raised Jesus from the dead.

Luke's story has its own distinctive emphases as do each of the other Gospel narratives. First, Jerusalem has special significance as the location for Jesus' resurrection and the birth of the church.

Second, Jesus' words to the women became the essential creedal statement of the church: "Why do you look for the living among the dead? He is not here, but has risen. Remember how he told you, while he was still in Galilee, that the Son of Man must be handed over to sinners, and be crucified, and on the third day rise again" (24:5-6). This is what the women believed; this is what Luke asks us to believe.

Third, the women in Luke's account reported to the disciples what they had experienced at the empty tomb; but their story was dismissed as "an idle tale" (verse 11). The disciples believed only when Jesus himself came to them on the road to Emmaus and in the room in Jerusalem.

In Matthew's resurrection account (Matthew 28:1-10), the risen Christ greets Mary Magdalene and the other Mary; while in John, Mary Magdalene discovers that the man she thinks is a gardener is actually the resurrected Jesus (John 20:11-18). Luke does not tell us that the women actually saw and spoke with Jesus following his resurrection; but unlike the women in Mark 16, who ran from the empty tomb in fear, the women in Luke spread the good news of the risen Christ. Luke may well be challenging his readers, including us today, to believe the Resurrection, whether we have seen and touched the risen Christ ourselves.

So what about us? Can we believe the account of Jesus' resurrection in today's Gospel reading? We have not experienced the risen Christ in the same way Jesus' first disciples did; yet if we open our hearts and minds, we can see the signs of the risen Christ among us. We appreciate the coming of spring and see in budding trees and blooming flowers signs of God-given life. Sometimes, however, we become so focused on the witness of nature at Easter—early dawns, bright flowers, and warm air—that we overlook the witness of God.

Our first appointment together was to seven churches in the mountains of North Carolina. Both of us had grown up in more temperate climates, with Easter Sundays warm enough for spring dresses and outdoor Easter egg hunts.

Our first Easter in the mountains took us by surprise. We awoke early on Easter Sunday that year and glanced out the window. We were shocked to find that the ground was covered with snow. Sally, who had grown up in Georgia, was especially confused. What were we supposed to do now? Should we shovel the snow off the church steps and go on with services as usual? Should we wear our heavy winter coats over our Easter outfits? Needless to say, that snowy morning we had to rethink our expectations of church on Easter Sunday.

The reason that we had gathered at church on Easter Sunday had absolutely nothing to do with the weather. We had gathered to declare that Jesus Christ is risen from the dead. While none of us could expect a warm, sunny day that particular Easter, we did expect at church that Easter Sunday the risen Christ would come and be present among us.

Today we read the account of Jesus' resurrection in Luke and give thanks. Because Jesus has been raised from the dead, we experience hope—hope that is ours whether the sun is shining and the flowers are blooming. Because Christ lives, we hope for life abundant; we hope for life eternal.

The ancient Greeks told another story about a king named Sisyphus. While he was alive, Sisyphus loved to trick others, so when he died,

Hades, the god of the underworld, decided to trick Sisyphus. At his death, Sisyphus was given the task of forcing a huge stone up a steep hill. Unfortunately, every time Sisyphus almost reached the top of the hill, the huge stone slipped from his hands and rolled all the way to the bottom again. The trick on Sisyphus turned out to be a tragedy. For all eternity, Sisyphus was condemned to push a boulder up a hill, not just once but over and over again. There was no getting rid of that huge stone.[3]

Today, on Easter Sunday, we declare to the world that there is no stone or boulder big enough to take away our hope for tomorrow.

The risen Christ is present with us, giving us the strength and energy to move any and all stones in our lives. All this is possible because the biggest stone of all has been moved away from Jesus' tomb. Christ is risen!

How do you experience the risen Christ in your life? What stones have been rolled away for you?

---

[1] See two versions of this story at *vcu.edu/engweb/webtexts/eurydice/eurydice myth.html.*

[2] *The United Methodist Book of Worship,* 371-72.

[3] From *mythweb.com/encyc/entries/sisyphus. html.*